M000304410

Turn
the
Page

Endorsements

Are you ready to change your life ... and turn the page for greater success? If you answered "Yes," then you need to read this dynamic book by Dr. Johnny Parker. Dr. Parker is an awesome teacher and incredible executive coach, who has assisted countless numbers of people in turning the page to a better future. Don't just read this book, study it ... and it will help you to do more, be more and achieve more!

—**Dr. Willie Jolley**, Best Selling Author of *A Setback Is A Setup For A Comeback and An Attitude of Excellence*

If you want to be the author of your own destiny—literally—Johnny Parker has much to offer. His goal in this thoughtful and well-written book is to help you to become the hero of your own life, actively engaged in creating your next chapter.

—**Marshall Goldsmith**, PhD executive coach, business educator and New York Times-bestselling author, ranked the number one leadership thinker in the world by Thinkers50

I am thrilled about Johnny Parker's *Turn the Page* for three reasons. I deeply like the humble and brilliant man who wrote it. This is Dr. Parker's magnum opus of coaching people and relationships. All of us can improve our life as we become proactive page turners.

—**Jeff Kemp**, former NFL quarterback, VP-FamilyLife, author Facing the Blitz

Turn the Page is a refreshing look at the congruency that must exist in a leader. It is a reminder to each one of us that leadership is work and to be a leader we must be committed to an inner integrity that both empowers us to lead and sustains us when we do.

—**Dr. Walter S. Thomas Sr., Pastor,** New Psalmist Baptist Church

Dr. Parker has a passion for seeing people live full and meaningful lives with purpose. *Turn the Page* is a book that leads others toward purposeful living in a distinct and practical way. Dr. Parker uses personal and professional stories, questions and exercises to lead the reader into self-discovery, through personal lies and hurdles, into dreams, purpose and legacy. Through storytelling and transparency, Dr. Parker creates vulnerability which draws the reader in and encourages personal risk and honesty.

—**Diane M. Wiater,** PhD, Adjunct Professor, Regent University, School of Business & Leadership

Wouldn't it be an awesome gift if you received some simple, but powerful, truth by which you could create a life that thrills your heart every single day? All of us want to live a life that has meaning, but too often we languish in sameness! You will need to read less than ten pages of this amazing book to pole vault out of "sameness." Your life will instantly take on new meaning, fresh excitement and a sense of hope!!! You will be moved into practical actions before you finish the first chapter. Give yourself this life-changing gift of wisdom! Read it and rise up into a new life experience. Don't wait to create a life with meaning!

—**Glenna Salsbury**, Professional Speaker, Author of *The Art of the Fresh Start*

If your life were a novel what would be your story? How would it end? What plot twists brought you to where you are today? These are the types of thought-provoking questions in *Turn the Page*, which will help you find the moral of your story and ultimately a life that is filled and fulfilled with purpose.

—**Michelle Singletary**, Nationally Syndicated Personal Finance Columnist, *The Washington Post*, Author of *The 21-Day Financial Fast.*

Turn the Page is one of the most practical life mapping tools I've seen in thirty years of working with leaders. Dr. Johnny Parker has crafted a series of steps to guide you in dreaming your story, and then designing your story to experience a powerful destiny. Anyone stuck in the confusion of life will benefit from one of America's most trusted executive coaches who comes alongside to help you become a "Page Turner" in this powerful book destined to become a personal growth classic.

> **—Dwight Bain,** author, Leadership Coach, media personality and founder of the LifeWorks Group in Florida

This is a tour-de-force in personal and professional development books. Dr. Parker combines honest self-disclosures with compelling strategies for achieving introspective awareness with the ultimate aim of pursuing renewed purpose, fulfillment, and meaning in life. *Turn the Page* helps readers make the transformation from living life as "bookmarks" that remain stuck and stagnant versus living as "page turners" who live intentionally by cultivating their talent, approaching life strategically, and more importantly, by nurturing their social, emotional and spiritual sense of self.

> **—Norma L. Day-Vines,** PhD,
> Professor-Counseling and Human Development,
> John Hopkins University School of Education

As an executive coach and leader, Dr. Johnny Parker has assisted hundreds if not thousands of people in turning the page in their lives toward a better future. Anyone who reads this book will be challenged to be and do their best as Johnny becomes just the mentor you've been waiting for!

> **—Dr. David Anderson,**
> *Real Talk with Dr. David Anderson* Radio Show

In life, we have so many roles, often changing daily, based on our position and relationship. It can be hard to see between everything we are for others and know who we really are as a person and who we want to be. When you don't know, and don't know how to know, read Dr. Parker's *Turn the Page*.

It takes you through so many real-life examples of people and stories we all know and to which we can relate.

One Storylie that especially resonated with me is "The More Storylie, or Less is More".

Learn how to be a Page Turner in your life stories as an individual, with your family, and in your profession. Read, and re-read, this book with your supporting casts!

—**Laurell Aiton,** Vice President, Human Resources, Smartronix

We owe a debt of gratitude to Dr. Johnny Parker for his excellent book, *Turn the Page*. He brings clarity and practicality to anyone who desires to have an impact. Whether you're a business leader, a sports leader, a family leader, or just want to be a better person, this book will give you inspiration and applications that can be used immediately.

—**Pat Richie**, Principal Consultant, The Table Group, Former Chaplain of the Super Bowl Champion San Francisco 49'ers, Author, *Wisdom for the Busy Leader*

I absolutely loved *Turn the Page*! As an entrepreneur and executive, I definitely strive to be a Page Turner every day! I strongly encourage all individuals and executives who are serious about self-development and desire to strengthen their professional and personal lives to read this book.

—**Charlisa R. Watson, MHSA,** President and CEO, CRW and Associates, LLC

In *Turn the Page*, Dr. Parker poignantly describes how we are able to recalibrate our lives toward purposeful direction by accepting who we are, while embracing the challenges of evolving into our best God-given selves. He details steps necessary to live our lives filled with substance, meaningfulness, and focused direction. This book is a profound "game changer" and illustrates the game plan for all of us working to get to the highest level personally and professionally.

—Necole Parker Green, Principal/CEO,
The ELOCEN Group and CEO Lux

In my work with leaders and marriages, especially faith-based ones, I'm continually amazed at the abject poverty of hope evident in their most vital relationships. Amid their endless busyness and plastered smiles, there is a deep emotional need to get more from their lives. I want to personally hand each of them Dr. Parker's *Turn the Page: Unlocking the Story Within You* to encourage them to see that within each of them is the power to bend the universe in their favor—not through new age mysticism but by expanding what they believe is possible. Rest assured, Dr. Parker's carefully crafted script promises them and you an adventure without equal. And, boy does it deliver!

—Dr. Harold Arnold, Jr., Leadership Enthusiast,
Family Life Podcaster, and Author of *The Unfair Advantage: A Grace-inspired Path to Winning at Marriage*

In *Turn the Page*, Dr. Parker lays out a framework necessary to pull back the layers of our life's story to uncover the truth of who God created us to be, do and have. It is with this truth that we can construct a meaningful story that manifests into a life of contribution, growth and contentment. In these pages, you get to uncover and embrace the depths of your story and in the end, turn the page to, as Dr. Parker says, live a great story filled with adventure that leaves others better off than how you found them.

—Stan & Chereace Richards, Authors and Entrepreneurs,
From the Bus to the Bentley, No More Limits, and
Faith. Focus. Action: The Journey to Becoming Who You Are

Turn
the
Page

UNLOCKING THE
STORY WITHIN
YOU

DR. JOHNNY PARKER

Elk Lake
PUBLISHING, INC.

Plymouth, Massachusetts

Copyright Notice

Turn the Page: Unlocking the Story Within You

First edition. Copyright © 2017 by Dr. Johnny C. Parker Jr. The information contained in this book is the intellectual property of Dr. Johnny C. Parker Jr. and is governed by the United States and International copyright laws. All rights reserved. No part of this publication, either text or image, may be used for any purpose other than personal use. Therefore, reproduction, modification, storage in a retrieval system, or retransmission, in any form or by any means, electronic, mechanical, or otherwise, for reasons other than personal use, except for brief quotations in reviews or articles and promotions, is strictly prohibited without prior written permission of the publisher.

Cover Design: Corinne Walker
Interior Design: Melinda Martin
Editors: Kathleen Peoples, Deb Haggerty
Published in Association with the Les Stobbe Agency

PUBLISHED BY: Elk Lake Publishing, Inc., 35 Dogwood Dr., Plymouth, MA 02360

Scripture taken from the New King James Version®. Copyright © 1982 by Thomas Nelson. Used by permission. All rights reserved.

Library Cataloging Data
Names: Parker, Jr., Dr. Johnny C. (Dr. Johnny C. Parker Jr.)
Turn the Page: Unlocking the Story Within You /Dr. Johnny C. Parker Jr.
162 p. 23cm × 15cm (9in × 6 in.)
Description: Elk Lake Publishing, Inc. digital eBook edition | Elk Lake Publishing, Inc. POD paperback edition | Elk Lake Publishing, Inc, Trade paperback edition | Elk Lake Publishing, Inc. Hardcover | Elk Lake Publishing, Inc. 2017.
Identifiers: ISBN-13: 978-1-944430-60-3| 978-1-944430-61-0 | 978-1-944430-62-7 | 978-1-946638-07-6
Key Words: 1. Personal Development, 2. Goals, 3. Community, 4. Renewal, 5. Your Story, 6. Bold Truth, 7. Quest
5087461734 2017 NF

Dedication

I dedicate this book to three people ...

To my bride and girlfriend, Lezlyn, who is a Page Turner and desires to help women write better stories and get their fight back. Thank you for allowing space for me to be vulnerable and for helping me unlock the story within me.

I also dedicate this book to Richard Pannell, President of BMRA (Business Management Research Associates, Inc.), who was enthusiastic about the message of this book and was the first CEO to give me an opportunity to share the material with leaders in corporate America. Richard, thank you for being a fan and a friend. You left this world too soon and I miss you.

To my assistant, Pat Jackson, who regularly anticipates what I need and works tirelessly to make me look great. You are one amazing woman!

Acknowledgments

In writing this book, I have come to realize that I can't know myself, grow myself, by myself. I have needed a community of family members and friends to challenge my thinking, encourage me to stay the course, and to simply pray for me.

To my sons: JP, Jordan, and Joel—Thank you for forgiving me when I have gotten it wrong as your dad. You are teaching me to do more listening than lecturing. Being a husband and dad have taught me about the power of vulnerability in building deep relationships. Thank you for being my teachers.

To my parents: Johnny and Gwen Parker and Kent and Doreen Miller (I have "in loves" not in laws)—Thank you for investing your prayers and your finances in helping to get the work of *Turn the Page* off the ground and running. The world is a tough place. A man needs fans to believe in him, especially in a world filled with rejection. You have been the wind beneath my wings when I didn't have any strength to flap. Thank you, Mom and Dad, for loving me, believing in me and encouraging me to keep flapping my wings and soar.

To: Zanise, Mitzi, Janelle, Taylor, Denzel, and Dexter—Thank you for being the best sister, sister-in-law, nieces, and nephews that a brother and uncle could ask for.

To my coaches and counselors: Dr. Mark Good and Dwight Bain—Every person needs a coach, counselor, or supportive friends to help them process life and its losses. You have walked with me through dark nights of my soul. Your wisdom, your encouragement, your friendship, and your listening ear gave me hope in moments of discouragement.

To: my Pastor John K. Jenkins Sr. and First Lady Trina Jenkins—You both epitomize the way of a Page Turner! Each week you literally help thousands turn the page to a hopeful and better story. You did it for my family when we were stuck in a bad story. We love you.

To: MFC Leaders and **Spiritual Cares**—Rickey McCullough, Darrel Spears, Skip Little, Reggie Alexander, Chris Streeter, Keith Honesty, Milton Holt, Alan Andrews, Roland Hawthorne, Jeff Barnett, Patrick Lamar, Chuck Dansby, Malcolm Williams, Bob Clark, Kenny McNeil, Carl Bartee, Mark Rhyns, Walt Harris, Norm Thomas, Darryn Hyman,

Giles Hagood, Lou Holder, Yvette Haley, and Rev. John Fortt—It is a privilege to serve alongside you to help men and women be better leaders, better parents, better spouses, and better people. Thank you for your patience and grace for the times I missed the mark as a leader. I am a better man and leader because of each of you.

To: Adrienne Alexander, Deron Snyder, and Dr. Harold Arnold—Thank you for endless conversations and for helping me in choosing the right words and language for this book.

To: Sheryl Smith, Dr. Shirley Turner, and Stacey Smith—Thank you for helping me facilitate at "Turn the Page" seminars and helping people live better stories.

To: Keith Wall and Kathleen Peoples—Thank you! This book could not have unfolded the way it has without your distinct perspectives. You both are absolutely magnificent in the art and craft of editing and book writing. It has been fun and easy working with you.

To: my agent, Les Stobbe, and my publisher, Deb Haggerty—Thank you for believing in this project and helping it get to the finish line.

Thank you to the Walker and Parker Family everywhere—Thank you for your prayers and encouragement. Corinne and Ben, you both have been simply terrific in the design work of the book and coloring book. It is always good when we can keep the work and the money in the family.

Thank you, Irv Clark, Chris Harrod, and Clarence Shuler—You men are my supporting cast. You guys have access to my backstage and have wept when I have wept and rejoiced when I rejoiced. Thank you for making it safe for me to be me.

Contents

Your Life Can Be a Page Turner

For a while, I felt stuck in a bad story. In the realm of relationships, a close friend had betrayed my trust. In the professional arena, I was downsized from a consulting job—one that had been the job of my dreams. I felt myself getting older and regretted I had not earned my doctorate much earlier in my life so I could be further ahead in my career. All of these events together culminated in the perfect storm—like a chapter of never-ending pain. I was bitter about life and angry with God. I wanted to strike out at someone or something. I began to live vicariously through reality TV. There were moments I wished I could trade my story for someone else's. I was languishing.

Have you ever been stuck in a bad story? Through the chapters of my life and my activities as a professional coach, I have discovered life requires regular processing, especially in a noisy world with lots of distractions and constant interruptions. So, at that difficult time, I had to ask myself, "How did I get here?"

First, a confession. For much of my life, I was content to live a good, safe, predictable existence. Don't get me wrong—I received a good education, carved out a good career, made good friendships, and had a good family. I earned a good income, enjoyed a good amount of respect from my peers, and engaged in lots of good activities.

Life was all good ... but not great.

I had swallowed whole the typical version of the American Dream: get a college degree, marry a nice person, establish a respectable career, sock money away in retirement accounts, buy a comfortable house in the suburbs, raise responsible children, and then retire at age sixty-five, with some energy left to hit the golf course or tennis court. That's life, right? Just get what you can and do what you are supposed to do, and join the masses—or perhaps get a tiny bit ahead of them. There's nothing wrong with that, is there? Not really—unless you sense somehow that there must be more to life.

For me, having a personal, specific, and unique dream for my life did not come naturally. I grew up playing it safe. I worked hard to gain security, and I succeeded, or so I thought. Not until I was thirty-five years old and working for a large nonprofit organization did I begin to realize safety and security are fine as far as they go ... they just don't go very far. At that time, I saw men and women in their early twenties start their own companies during the dot.com boom of the 1990s. They had a dream, and they pursued their dream. They had an idea, and they nurtured that idea. They felt a calling, and they acted on their calling.

I thought to myself, "They can't do that! They need permission. They need more experience. They need more years under their belt. They need to slow down, they should be more responsible and play it safe!" But perhaps my indignation was rooted in envy.

In the last decade, I have had at least three aha moments in my life. During that experience of envy, I realized that I must give myself permission to change, to act, to dream. This was, I am happy to announce, the first of my aha moments about viewing my life as a story. I began to understand that I was the writer of my life story, but and so far, I was churning out standard, ho-hum fare. More and more, I felt an urge, a prodding to fulfill my God-given potential, aim higher, and strive for a vibrant, meaningful life. I challenged myself to release the parking brakes of complacency and shortsightedness and go full throttle toward the adventure of living. In essence, I knew I had to turn the page—to make dramatic changes—for the rest of my life story to move from languishing to flourishing. By flourishing, I don't refer to emotional bliss or elation, but rather to adopting a mindset of growth and living with a sense of calling and purpose.

In the chapters ahead, I will share more of my personal story and the elements involved in turning the page in your life. Be advised I have not followed these steps perfectly. I work actively to disentangle myself from unproductive plotlines. Moreover, I tell you up front that 'turning the page' in your life is a daily process, not a one-time event. For true authorship, each of us must be purposeful and choose how to set the stage and direct the action on any given day. For example, I ask myself, "Will I make my story today about caring for others or will I stay stuck in how someone disappointed me yesterday?" Most days I have to steer my heart toward a fresh page of speaking kind words and doing good deeds in spite of how I feel.

Now let me shift the focus to you. Does any part what I describe resonate with you? Maybe you have reached a point where you feel a hunger for something more. Perhaps you've started saying things like:

"I feel like I am just existing, not really living."

"I thought I would be farther ahead by this time."

"Why does my life feel so full yet so empty?"

"I have accomplished a lot but still feel unsatisfied."

"I know I should be doing something different—but what?"

"I'm doing lots of good things, but I'm not clear about my purpose."

"I want to be more and do more."

If any of these statements sound familiar, you're likely feeling stuck, unchallenged, and disillusioned in your current chapter of life. The script you are living is not the gripping storyline you imagined for your life. In short, you are eager—perhaps desperate—to turn the page, to create a life story full of meaning, adventure, and lasting impact. You want your story to move from lackluster to a blockbuster.

The Path of a Page Turner

I initially set out to write a book for leaders in the workplace. Then I recalled my second aha moment, which occurred during my doctoral studies when I was studying great leaders and striving to build a strong family. I realized leadership at work mirrors leadership at home; they share the same dynamics. Leadership at work and at home both involve building relationships, trust, integrity, strengths; having courageous conversations, vision, core values, culture, emotional intelligence, morale, and creating a legacy. As Jon Acuff says, "If you lead on stage and not at home, you're an actor, not a leader."

You lead from who you are. Leadership does not require a fancy title or a corner office. You can't simply put on a leadership hat when you walk into an office building. Leadership does not take place from nine to five—leadership happens 24/365 and stems from your unique sphere of influence and how you serve others.

Parents are leaders, coaches are leaders, and teachers are leaders. Leadership is a series of relationship opportunities. All businesses are people businesses. All organizations are made up of people. And every day, your life, your home, leadership, business, and community activities combine to tell a story.

For the purposes of this book, I have coined a new term: The Page Turner. A Page Turner is someone who does the common thing in an uncommon way and experiences uncommon results.

- Page Turners are leaders who courageously pursue the best version of themselves regardless of the effort.

- Page Turners realize that living a great story happens intentionally, not automatically. No one wanders toward living a powerful story. Page Turners are deliberate about how they show up each day.

- Page Turners seek to live, love, and lead from the heart and soul, or what I call the "backstage." The "frontstage" is the surface that the public sees—accomplishments, productivity, and presentation. The "backstage" is the private world that focuses on motives, values, and purpose. With this as their aim, Page Turners flourish and don't languish. Page Turners have grit. They possess the passion and perseverance for long-term goals. Page Turners realize that in addition to talent and IQ, effort and the cultivation of character strengths (e.g. humility, compassion, and kindness) are important for living an impactful life.

- Page Turners Clarify Their Quest. They choose the story they want their life to tell.

- Page Turners Demand Bold Truth. They fearlessly own both their challenges and strengths.

- Page Turners Champion Generosity. They seek to leave others better off than how they found them.

- Page Turners Engage Community. They have a supporting cast. They realize they can't know themselves or grow themselves, by themselves.

- Page Turners Pursue Continual Renewal and thus nurture and sustain themselves.

- Page Turners explore their unique strengths to serve a purpose greater than themselves. A Page Turner realizes if their life dream features only them as the star, that dream can turn into a nightmare.

- Page Turners seek to notice and appreciate the positive in the world. They focus on gratitude and acknowledge what works.

Page Turners do understand, however, that life follows indirect or zigzag paths. Like a river, life meanders and flows over rocks and diversions rather than proceeding in a straight line ... it is not linear. Page Turners have figured out that life can walk three steps forward and two steps back. However, accepting there are reversals and challenges in life is not the same as accepting stagnancy. Page Turners do not allow themselves to become Bookmarks.

Bookmarks are passive. When a reader inserts a paper bookmark in a novel, they turn away to attend to other things that take precedence. The flow in the action of the book is stopped. Similarly, a Bookmark lets other people take precedence in the life they want to lead. They may allow themselves to be placed wherever other people see fit. Bookmarks minimize their own power to control their lives and are controlled by others. Bookmarks mark space and time and don't move forward —they can be all talk and no "show."

As an aspiring Page Turner, you avoid being a bookmark when you refuse to give another person the rights to your life. You go beyond dwelling on what you were in the past and only talking about your dreams. Whereas Bookmarks stand still, Page Turners are active. You can leave passive bookmarking behind and become a dynamic Page Turner.

Are you ready to be a Page Turner? Are you ready to live your most powerful, influential, meaningful story? Good news— you've come to the right place. Turn the Page will equip you to dream and envision what your impact can become, design your lifestyle to create transformation, and chart a destiny for ongoing influence and impact. Prepare to make your story an exhilarating Page Turner, like a book when you can't wait to see what happens next.

Chapter One

What's Your Story?

"There is no agony like bearing an
untold story inside you."

Maya Angelou

Many people feel stuck in a disappointing story. Perhaps not their whole story—maybe a chapter in the story is less than ideal. Some are in suspense; they face the mystery of trying to figure out who they are and what they really want for their life. Others endure the drama of processing pain and confronting challenges. Then for others, their life is a horror story, discovering what fears they allow to hold them hostage.

Speaking of mystery and suspense, as with most people, birthdays ending with "0" hit me hard. When we arrive at these milestones (3-0, 4-0, 5-0, 6-0), we're compelled to reflect, evaluate, and contemplate. We assess what we've accomplished so far—and how much more we want to achieve. We pause to take the measure of our days. As the philosopher, Soren Kierkegaard said, "Life can only be understood backward, but it must be lived forward."

I was certainly in this frame of mind when I turned the big 4-0. Here's where my third aha moment occurred. A few weeks before the big day, my wife, Lezlyn, asked what birthday gift I wanted. She suggested the latest electronic gadget or maybe new golf clubs. She offered to make my favorite meal—honey-glazed chicken and strawberry shortcake.

"What I really want this year," I told her, "is to spend a few days at Ocean City on my own. Walk on the beach. Enjoy peace and quiet. Have unhurried time to think, pray, and reflect. Listen to the surf as I journal." She knew I had often seemed lost in thought leading up to this birthday, so she was happy to grant my wish—and promised to make my favorite meal another time.

Soon, I found myself with three days of solitude. I spent long hours walking, journaling, reading and reflecting. To some people, this respite from my usual activities might sound like no big deal, maybe even boring. But those days helped me realize that for most of the previous decade I had been sprinting through life as urgently as the runners chased by the bulls in Pamplona, Spain. I'd been raising three kids, tending to my marriage, leading church ministries, completing degrees, speaking all over the country, traveling internationally ... and getting more and more exhausted, wearing myself out.

In fact, by the time I reached the ripe old age of 40, I felt burned out and depressed. During my Ocean City getaway, I thought: "Why have I done all this—really? I've accomplished lots of good things, but for what exactly? What am I aiming for? Will I ever stop wrestling with the need for validation from other people? Am I speeding toward a finish line that doesn't exist?"

The Power of Our Stories

Think of someone with an amazing story.
Perhaps that person is a speaker you heard at a retreat or workshop. You were riveted with the details of his modest beginnings, the obstacles he overcame, and the successes he has attained since then. Or maybe the person has written a powerful memoir. Reading her story, you can't believe the epic hardships and plot twists she endured to become who she is today.

Then again, who says the story that grabs you must be that of a "real" person? Perhaps you thought immediately of a fictional story told through the eyes of a movie director, an epic tale that no matter how many times you see it, you are compelled by the wrenching emotion, the vivid characters, and the triumphant resolution. You might even be known among your friends for frequently quoting your favorite lines from this movie.

Of course, who doesn't love a good story? In fact, people of every age and stage in life are drawn to stories. Always have been. Always will be. That's why, when bedtime rolls around, kids don't ask for statistics; they ask to hear a story. According to psychologist Jerome Bruner, facts are twenty times more likely to be remembered if they are part of a story. Organizational psychologist Peg Neuhauser found similar results in her work with corporations, explaining, "Learning derived from a well-told story is remembered more accurately and for far longer than the learning derived from facts or figures." That's why history students bemoan the need to learn endless names and dates, but they fall in love with history when their teacher is a great storyteller. Public speakers—from presidents to preachers—understand audiences remember compelling anecdotes more than anything else.

In the words of best-selling novelist Janet Litherland, "Stories have power. They delight, enchant, touch, teach, recall, inspire, motivate, challenge. They help us understand. They imprint a picture on our minds. Want to make a point or raise an issue? Tell a story."

Stories explain where we have been. They point to where we are going. They connect the dots between seemingly random experiences and events, creating patterns that make sense in a world that often doesn't. Stories make abstract ideas memorable. They engage our emotions as well as our intellect. They connect us to each other, bridging gaps in age, race, beliefs, and experience.

Stories are the most powerful ways to convey who we are, what we do, and why we do what we do. High-impact people and the best leaders soon realize that everyone has a story and we should invest energy in each one—including our own.

Your Story Matters

You, my friend, are in the process of writing your own amazing story. You may not be a public speaker or a famous writer (and I'm pretty sure you're not a fictional hero!), but you are creating your own epic tale even now. Every day, your life is made up of episodes that accumulate to tell a story. Individual moments, whether breathtaking or banal, are strung together like scenes from a novel or on a movie reel, and they compose the story of, well ... you.

Life proceeds moment-by-moment, day-by-day. You live your story one scene, one page at a time. Poet Annie Dillard says, "How we spend our days is, of course, how we spend our lives." This current season of your life matters immensely, and this season is made up of an endless string of "mini-seasons" called weeks, days, hours, and moments.

Your story began with "once upon a time" as you entered life and has progressed from there. Just as in any good tale, your story undoubtedly contains zany characters, plots twists, suspense, romance, heroes, villains, and perhaps even a cliffhanger or two. There are two great events in your life: the day you are born, and the day you discover why you were born. Clarifying your quest, your reason for being on earth, will empower you to live each day with purpose and precision.

A Great Story Needs Strategic Editing

When you perceive your life as an unfolding story, you can embrace a principle foundational to every powerful, persuasive tale: a great story benefits from careful, calculated, and sometimes ruthless editing. A good storyteller knows which events deserve attention and which should be minimized or even ignored altogether. Whether outlining a speech, writing a book, or making a movie, the storyteller knows that not every scene deserves to be memorialized, and that many scenes—even good ones—end up deleted or on the cutting room floor.

When a French newspaper erroneously reported the death of Alfred Nobel, the chemist who invented dynamite, he read his own obituary. Alfred's brother Ludwig was who actually died, but the newspaper published Alfred's obituary and referred to him as "the merchant of death." The title disturbed Alfred deeply, and he decided to edit his life story. From that point on, he chose to use his wealth to create a prize honoring people who foster peace in the world. That's how the Nobel Peace Prize was born.

Thinking of your life as a story allows you to do the same thing, to be intentional about what you want to include and exclude. The most compelling stories are not mindless collections of random scenes and events; they have been carefully edited to include only what is most important to advance the narrative while deleting things that distract from the greater purpose. Our lives should follow suit.

A Great Story Pivots on the Choices of its Characters

In viewing your life as a story, you can embrace a second principle of great storytelling: Every memorable story is propelled by the choices of its primary character. Great stories might begin with random events that impact the wellbeing of the main character. But at some point—and we've all watched enough movies and read enough books to know how this works—the main characters stop being tossed to and fro by events they didn't choose or create. They start making choices and taking actions to solve problems, reinvent their lives, or change their identity.

In the story of your life, the primary character is, of course, you.

Are you being fiercely purposeful in living out the story you want to create with the days you have been given? Are your years on earth composing the story you truly want to tell? In my role as an executive coach, speaker, and author, I meet people every day who feel buffeted by haphazard events in life. They don't know why certain things keep happening to them. They can't figure out why they experience failure after failure. They are convinced they are victims. Although they long to change their stories, they don't feel they have the power to do so. They believe they're being called to do something greater but lack the courage to step out and make something happen. They may even grieve over the way their story is unfolding. I have heard more than once the tragic lament, "I never thought my life would turn out this way."

People often forget they are the ones who have the power to play author and editor of their own novel, focusing on events and attitudes that will take them where they want to go, and casting aside the things that hold them back. They don't realize each day presents a chance to choose and act in ways that will change the end of the book; that every day is a chance to write their life story with a different perspective, in a different voice, leading to a different end.

For many years, this sense of powerlessness was my wife's narrative. Growing up, Lezlyn felt as if she were only an actress on the stage of her own life, while well-meaning people backstage fed her lines about how to dress, talk, where to go to school and what to believe. Despite their good intentions, their script did not fit the desires of Lezlyn's heart. Only with lots of soul searching and coaching did Lezlyn begin speaking her own lines and writing her own story.

A Great Story Shows Us the Big Picture

Do you know that when we change the end of the story, we change the significance of everything that has happened leading up to that ending? When the fictional hero saves the world, all the lost battles leading up to the final victory cease to look like failures and start to look like stepping stones.

When someone has an epiphany that helps them reinvent their life, all the struggles and setbacks leading up to that moment of insight cease to look like disasters and start to look like lessons well learned. When someone stops being a victim and starts taking steps to reclaim their life, all the hurts experienced up to that moment cease to look like tragedies and start to look like the very things that made them stronger than they thought they could be.

If you're like me, you marvel at the way some people's stories come together. Hindsight and reflection allow us to put seemingly random events in our lives—even hardships and hurts—into a context that makes sense. The long view allows us to piece together disparate parts into a cohesive whole. Remembering there is a big picture can make all the difference in how the rest of your story unfolds. Taking charge of your life now can put even the most difficult past in a whole new light.

I consider Dr. Lonise Bias a mentor and friend. You may recall she is the mother of Len Bias, who was set to become a star in the NBA. The day after he was drafted by the Boston Celtics, Len took cocaine and died instantly. Len's death shocked the country and began the "War on Drugs." As if her son's death wasn't enough for this mother to bear, a year later another son, Jay, was shot and killed.

Dr. Bias and I used to work out at the same fitness center. Between running on the treadmill and lifting weights, we engaged in penetrating conversations about life and purpose. During these talks, I remembered how my grandfather frequently said: "You can't holler and swallow at the same time." Another way of saying, "You can't speak and listen simultaneously." So, when Dr. Bias spoke, I listened carefully. I had a front-row seat to wisdom. On one occasion, she told me, "I tell audiences all the time that my two sons were two seeds that went down into the ground to bring forth life. That's what I believe. I was kicked into my purpose." Dr. Bias chose to recast her tragedies and turned the page to move forward. She became a public activist in the War on Drugs, concentrating her efforts in working with young people and fostering the self-esteem that inoculates them against the pressure to experiment with harmful substances.

Turning the page in your story is not always smooth and clean—in fact, most often change is messy. But turning the page can be magnificent and well worth the effort. A new story requires a fierce commitment to vulnerability. A team-bonding exercise underlined this point for me. The members of this group worked for the same company yet barely knew each other. The meeting was to help them work on a key project. To bring them together, I asked the group to form a circle and share one of their proudest life moments. Clearly, none of them wanted to be there. They were slow to stand up; their body language suggested imminent flight; there were frequent, pained glances toward the door.

Yet as they finally started, not one of the group members shared anything about work. They shared personal and vulnerable stories, such as overcoming domestic violence, watching the way a spouse cared for a dying mother, telling the family of their same-sex attraction, marrying a high school sweetheart fifty years later, being an introvert and finding the courage to speak to a crowd. Sharing this level of vulnerability and wading through these messy feelings together set the stage for trust and quality work among group members. Afterward, the group was transformed. There were smiles, nods, genuine eye contact, even tears. People who were usually quiet spoke up with ideas; there was laughter and a marked improvement in productivity.

The deeper your vulnerability, the deeper the human connection and trust. Your story is never more alive than when you are vulnerable. However, if you are like me, this rocks your boat. Exposing vulnerability is risky and unnatural. But here's the question: What is the alternative? Isolation? Avoidance? In the words of Dr. Phil, "How's that working for you?" The truth is, emotional isolation kills and vulnerability heals. Vulnerability is the pencil, and your heart is the page. Inscribing the pains and truths in our lives, instead of trying to erase them, informs and educates us and allows our full story to be written.

Let me share with you the five essential challenges of turning the page in your life:

To **Demand Bold Truth** means being truthful about the inadequate and inauthentic aspects of your story. You must be thoroughly honest about the areas you try to hide and the strengths you downplay. You must be brave enough to acknowledge your shortcomings without diminishing your attributes. Dare to take responsibility for your life. No blame. No minimizing. Own your story.

To **Clarify Your Quest** requires you to become vulnerable because clarification means fighting to be a voice and not an echo. Clarifying your quest empowers you and means deciding what story you want your life to tell, what your purpose is, and constructing your own self-definition. In every movie, the protagonist wants something. Playing it safe and following the pack is easy. As a Page Turner, you weren't born merely to fit in and go with the flow but to live an original story and aim for your specific goals.

To **Champion Generosity** means actively serving others. The Page Turner, that is the hero of the story, endeavors to leave the people in their story better off than how they found them without demanding anything in return. This makes the whole story better because we discover joy as we serve others. Yet, this brings risks because others may exploit your kindness. You will not always be appreciated. You may even be accused of having ulterior motives. Dare to be kind and giving anyway.

To **Engage Community** means you invite other people to shape your story. The protagonist never reaches their destiny without a supporting cast consisting of a mentor, coach, or friend. You may be tempted to isolate your heart. However, as a Page Turner, you can't know yourself or grow yourself by yourself. Allowing safe men and women with an objective view to hold you accountable is critical for a meaningful story. Yes, you can risk betrayal because although some people will be nurturing, a few could be poisonous—but you must remain willing to forgive. Dare to invest in relationships anyway.

To **Pursue Continual Renewal** requires you to sustain yourself while you sustain your impact. The Page Turner is deliberate about self-care and breathing margin in their backstage world. To prevent losing your way, recharging and recalibrating are essential. Intentional renewal is challenging because you can fear the time you take decreases your forward momentum. You may be reluctant to take a break lest opportunities pass you by. Others may deem you lazy or not a team player. Nevertheless, dare to renew; choose to live fully and nurture yourself as the writer of your own story.

I say again: Every day and every week, you are writing the story of your life. If you don't like how that story is turning out, don't despair. Your story is not finished. The chapters are not complete. You can revise the script to change the scenes ahead and most of all, how the story ends. Even better, you are the lead character in the book of your life, and your power to turn the page and move in an entirely new direction is far greater than you could imagine.

A Story Comes to Life

In the movie, *Jerry Maguire*, the main character is a greedy sports agent who later has a change of heart about his business. He visits the hospital where one of his clients, a professional football player, is recovering from a serious injury. Jerry encounters the player's son there, who questions a society that pays people big money to play sports and risk their lives. The boy begs Jerry to persuade his father to stop playing football.

Though exuding his usual aplomb, Jerry is deeply troubled by the conversation. Late that night, Jerry can't sleep. As the narrator, he says, "I hated myself. No, here's what it was. I hated my place in the world. I had so much to say and no one to listen." He begins drafting a mission statement, a treatise on how the sports agency should change. He urges agents to be less concerned about money and more concerned about the lives of their clients.

Jerry is unprepared for the firestorm his statement unleashes and the scorn he suddenly receives. After being fired for his convictions, Jerry lives out his newfound beliefs by starting his own company and vows to treat star athletes less like commodities and more like human beings.

He reflects, "Suddenly I was my father's son again. I remembered the simple pleasures of the job, how I ended up here out of law school, the way a stadium sounds when one of my players performs well on the field, the way we were meant to protect them in health and in injury. I remembered the words of the original sports agent, my mentor, the great Dicky Fox, who said, 'The key to this business is personal relationships.'" Jerry concludes, "It was the me, I'd always wanted to be."

That scene is a powerful scene in a powerful, thought-provoking movie. Maybe you, like Jerry, are in need of

that

aha moment, an epiphany that will change the trajectory of your story. Jerry looked back at his past and knew he had lost his true calling. What about your past have you lost that needs to be recovered? What do you harken back to that needs to be reclaimed? In what ways can your long-lost dreams, convictions, and beliefs be recaptured and reformulated to ensure that your story is as thrilling and powerful as possible?

The Point of the Story

- A great story needs strategic editing

- A great story pivots on the choices of its characters

- A great story shows us the big picture

- Page Turners Demand Bold Truth—they fearlessly accept ownership of challenges and strengths

- Page Turners Clarify Their Quest—they choose the story they want their life to tell

- Page Turners Exhibit Champion Generosity—they leave others better off

- Page Turners Engage Community—they have a supporting cast

- Page Turners Pursue Continual Renewal—they sustain themselves through renewing themselves

Your Developing Story

Have you ever kept a journal? My thirty years of journaling has provided high-definition clarity in my thinking, helping me feel I am living and feel like I am living actively, intentionally, and not merely existing.

1. Begin writing the pages of your life by journaling. Note three to five specific moments of gratitude throughout your day. You can choose to do this at the start or close of your day. Journaling daily gratitude puts your brain and your life on a positive trajectory.

2. After journaling gratitude, consider the question, "What am I discovering about me, relationships, leadership, and life?" Write your thoughts in your journal.

Chapter Two

Backstage—Where Your Story Originates

"Attend to your heart with all diligence
for out of it flow the issues of life."

Hebrew Proverb

In my mid-30s, I was driven to be successful, but my life was out of balance. I was working for a large nonprofit organization, leading counseling and development activities. I was sleeping too little, eating carelessly and too often, and had spotty communication with my wife.

In movie genre vernacular, my story was a blend of mystery and drama. I felt scattered, and the pages of my life had blown all over the place. There's a reason for this. Even though I am a deeply spiritual person and my faith has always guided my decision making, for a long time, I had focused primarily on my public world rather than my private world. My top priorities had become achievement, performance, and significance. In short, I had become a "human doing" instead of a "human being."

This distinction is important for all of us because our story— the real story—originates behind the curtains. If you have ever attended a theater production, you know there are two sections of the stage—the frontstage and the backstage. I will use this metaphor to illustrate how crucial both stages working in coordination with each other is. However, I will place unique focus on the backstage to make a point, as you will see shortly.

What is the Frontstage?

The frontstage is your public world—what is visible to others. This is the stage of performance. Others see how you "show up" at work, how you treat others, how you speak, and how you respond when dealing with difficulties and with difficult people. The frontstage is the surface everyone sees. This is also the stage of achievement, results, productivity, and profit. Please do not misunderstand me—the frontstage is vitally important. The frontstage determines how we measure progress, evaluate outcomes, and earn a living. However, the problem is most of our education and our culture emphasizes the frontstage solely. We start early influencing our kids' stories when we ask those questions such as, "What do you want to be when you grow up?" Of course, there is nothing wrong with this question, but it is one-sided. Our lives are not lived on the frontstage only. We should also encourage their perception and recognition of an inside world. "What was best about today?" "Did anything make you sad or glad today?

Yet I realize that to ask in conversation with leaders and high achievers, "How is your soul? What's going on deep within you?" is not the norm. The frontstage grabs our attention because what we do there is observable and quantifiable. In June 2016, I heard Brad Lomenick, the former director of Catalyst, one of the largest leadership conferences in North America, give a talk to teens. He told them advice he wished he'd received as a young person. "I wish someone had told me to focus on 'who' before 'do.'" In other words, let who you are becoming take center stage. Let that growth lead. Let becoming shape what you do.

Just as the surgeon general warns of danger on packs of cigarettes and bottles of alcohol, the frontstage should be handled with caution. As important as the frontstage is, the surface persona can easily become something it was never intended to be. I have coached many people who allowed their frontstage experience to define their worth and identity. As a result, they became driven. They were consumed with image management, hoping to convince others that they had everything all figured out. Having drive is necessary to fuel our accomplishments, to move us toward our calling. But when we become driven, something else is going on. Driven people can easily use frontstage pursuits to cover and attempt to heal backstage wounds like childhood abandonment and abuse. Frontstage-driven people risk gaining the world and losing their soul. They can wound others in their unbridled hunt for significance. As your heart and soul (your backstage) are nurtured—or not—the visible, frontstage aspects of your life will follow suit. Sustaining frontstage productivity depends on an intentional cultivation of your backstage.

What is the Backstage?

Simply put, the backstage is your essence, the real you. The backstage is the birthplace of your motives, values, vulnerability, and purpose—your private world. Backstage is the platform where your life is processed. The scenes and acts you live out on life's frontstage are generated backstage in your heart and soul, the deepest part of who you are.

There are challenges in managing our backstage: although you can't measure the losses, the soul's deterioration and malnourishment will surely become evident over time. A person can appear externally strong, but a breeze of adversity or sudden stressor will easily reveal internal instability. An unattended backstage leads to a messy frontstage.

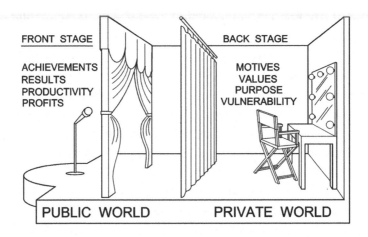

FRONT STAGE

ACHIEVEMENTS
RESULTS
PRODUCTIVITY
PROFITS

BACK STAGE

MOTIVES
VALUES
PURPOSE
VULNERABILITY

PUBLIC WORLD   PRIVATE WORLD

In my thirties, I downplayed my backstage. Motivated by fear of failure, I chased recognition and significance. Don't get me wrong; I believe in healthy ambition, that is, ambition focused on serving others. But my objectives were different then. My ambition and dreams had run amuck. The result showed in my marriage and produced panic attacks, controlling behavior, and chronic discontent. I was stuck in a bad story.

In 1998, I flew to a different city almost every weekend for speaking engagements and often woke up in a hotel bed not knowing what city I was in. The last event of that year was in Colorado, and I boarded the plane to Colorado Springs on a Thursday night with tears in my eyes. I didn't want to go because I was so physically exhausted, spiritually adrift, and emotionally spent. My speaking dates were going well, but that was not enough somehow. How could I accomplish so much good yet feel so bad? What was I chasing? Who was I trying to impress? Asking and answering those questions was a vital part of turning the page in my own life. This crisis is what led to my birthday on the beach when I began to edit my storyline. I looked at the questions for the decades of my life that had gone before, and how I wanted to be able to answer the questions in the future.

I saw there are backstage questions that we think privately in each decade.

- In our twenties, we ask:

  "Who am I?"
  "What do I really want?"

- In our thirties, we ask:

  "How can I do as much as I can, go as fast as I can, to be as successful as I can?"

- In our forties, we ask:

  "Am I there yet?"
  "What's missing in my life?"
  "Why am I not where I thought I would be at this point in my life?"

- In our fifties and sixties, we ask:

  "What will my legacy be?
  "How will I be remembered?"

- In our seventies and beyond, we ask:

  "Do I still have value?"
  "Does anyone remember what I once was?"
  "How do I use my acquired wisdom to bless others?"

The questions listed for the thirties were what I had been grappling with and what led to my aha moments at my birthday beach retreat. I thought forward to my final chapter; how would my story read? What would be said of me on my deathbed? What would my epitaph emphasize? I realized I wanted people to say I was successful because I invested in what mattered—

my marriage, my sons, and my friends. This meant changing. I became intentional about sharing my vulnerabilities with my wife and my sons—by being authentic about my needs and desires in nurturing the loves in my life. Doing this would re-write my story. And I extended this intentionality to my work, the process shaped my sense of calling and clarified my quest. Gradually my front stage and backstage came more into sync. I became more deliberate in preventing my front stage from smothering my backstage and creating meaning in my life story.

Your Storyline

Like a movie, your life has a plot—driven by your desires (what do you want?), a setting (when and where does your story take place?), characters (who are your key relationships and how are they shaping you?), and obstacles (how are you responding to conflict and adversity along the journey?). Your life will result in either triumph or tragedy depending on your choices. Are you ready for this? The surprise is your storyline is shaped backstage.

If your story or plot line for success has little or no space for love and vulnerability, then change your story. A new generation of people, including leaders in business and pro sports, has allowed words like love, compassion, spirit, heart, story, and soul to emerge as themes in their storyline. Acknowledging love and vulnerability are essential for turning the page toward a story worth living.

Dr. Humberto Maturana teaches the "biology of business" to leaders. He describes the meaning of work and how love is essential to business. In 1998, he was invited to the Massachusetts Institute of Technology (MIT) to present his paper: "The Biology of Business: Love Expands Intelligence." Here is an excerpt:

"If you look at any story of corporate transformation ... you will see that it is a story of love. Most problems in companies are not solved through competition, not through fighting, not through authority. They are solved through the only emotion that expands creativity ... Love expands intelligence and enables creativity. Love returns autonomy and, as it returns autonomy, it returns responsibility and the experience of freedom."

When I speak of love, I refer to a commitment to the greater good for another person and for an organization. We have entered a time when people are searching for deeper meaning in their lives and have grown disillusioned with possessions and a sole focus on the frontstage. These attitudes are radically changing the workplace, the marketplace, and the very heart of capitalism. Increasingly, today's most successful companies are now introducing backstage matters—love, authenticity, vulnerability, empathy, and mindfulness into their businesses. Costco, Commerce Bank, Wegmans, Starbucks, and Whole Foods now purpose to deliver emotional, experiential, and social value—not just profits.

Similarly, living your best story occurs through love and vulnerability. To be vulnerable is to be real and authentic. Being vulnerable means sharing ideas even though they might be ridiculed and summoning the courage to forgive someone who has hurt you. You can't step out and 'dare greatly' without vulnerability.

When people come to me for coaching, they often are seeking help integrating backstage with frontstage. When the backstage is ignored, addictions arise, health declines, and we lose our way. Becoming a Page Turner means becoming the best version of yourself. This means your backstage and frontstage should work in tandem. Page Turning is that simple and also that challenging. People looking to maximize their performance must be aware of the distinction between their backstage and frontstage. The frontstage is their Behavior Quotient (BQ): striving, achievements, appearance, attitude, and networking. The backstage is their Emotional Quotient (EQ): identity, mindfulness, motives, self-awareness, stress, and wellness.

Many people minimize the importance of these backstage elements. In fact, research shows that ninety percent of high performers have a high EQ or emotional intelligence. Fifty-eight percent of your work behavior demands emotional intelligence, and people with high EQ earn on average $29,000 more per year than those who lack it. Deliberate and balanced focus on the BQ and EQ leads to what I call the GQ or the Greatness Quotient.

A Healthy Backstage Leads to A Successful Frontstage

Are you familiar with the field of Positive Psychology? This is the scientific study of human strengths and optimal human functioning. Concepts such as happiness, gratitude, flourishing, flow, resilience, grit, and optimism are researched, and the results are applied to everyday life. In my Introduction to Positive Psychology course at Johns Hopkins University, I have observed the energy produced when my students approach their backstage with a positive mindset.

As a Page Turner, you can realize the power of the backstage by being intentional about how you power up, reset, and power down each day. To live an ordered backstage does not mean being perfect. But it does mean being perfectly honest when we fall short. Richard Rohr said in an interview with Oprah, "People require regular intervals of silence, rest, and daily touchstones to live from the soul, the true self, apart from living from a place of role and title."

Powering Up

Last summer on vacation, I did impromptu interviews with people whom I felt embodied the Page Turner ideal. I asked,

"What are the daily habits that prepare your backstage for frontstage success?"

- Daniel, who works for a national rental car company in Ohio, relies on reading inspirational books and meditating to start his day.

- Juan runs a high-end restaurant in Orlando. He says he starts the day sharing gratitude with his wife, exercising, and visualizing how he plans to show up as a kind, accessible leader to his staff.

For me, time in the great outdoors powers me up. Near my home, there are woodlands and a stream. Walking there is my "morning caffeine." There, I remind myself of my identity as God's child and being loved by God and created for influence. Prayer and being outdoors is like my dressing room; I imagine clothing myself in virtues. I speak words of affirmation over my life as I pray aloud that I will show up as a man, husband, dad, leader, and friend. I prepare myself to offer compassion, kindness, humility, gentleness, patience, forgiveness, and love. Doing this is not a magic formula for success. But the practice does set my heart on a positive trajectory in the morning that continues throughout my day.

Reset

After conducting a seminar for leaders in a sports organization, I met with Larry, one of the executives. Halfway through our meeting, his phone began sounding alerts. I assumed this was his way of notifying anyone in his office the meeting was over. I said, "I guess you have another appointment."

His reply surprised me: "Yes, I do, and it is with myself. Each afternoon at three o'clock I pause to check in with myself. I ask myself three questions: What am I feeling? How am I relating to people? What's important now?"

All of us need a reset mechanism or routine throughout the day and during the week. We must be intentional about checking in with ourselves and re-establishing our course if we have steered off track.

Powering Down

Executive coach Marshall Goldsmith, who consults for several Fortune 500 CEOs, recommends we review our day every evening before bed as a way of blending frontstage and backstage. He evaluates his goals and his emotional state. I encourage you to ask yourself growth-centered questions to foster personal development and nurture your potential. Admittedly, I'm still a work in progress in how I power down. Since I am at my best in the morning, I am accustomed to powering up without much of an issue. But after reading Marshall Goldsmith's wise suggestion, I am challenged to improve my game. Even in the act of creation, God powered down at the end of each day by reviewing His work and assessing that work as good.

I now use the following six questions to power down. The list addresses areas where I want to grow and avoid regression. My friends Clarence and Chris also regularly ask me the questions below. Knowing these men will keep me accountable spurs me to live with greater awareness and intentionality.

- What inspired and refreshed me today?

- Did I meditate, reflect, and spend time with God today?

- What good work of mine am I most proud of today?

- Did I cherish my wife and affirm my sons today?

- Was I present with people rather than distracted by technology today?

- Was I authentic and courageous today?

Studies from positive psychology emphasize a variety of virtues: wisdom (creativity, big-picture view), courage (valor, integrity), humanity (love, kindness), justice (leadership, teamwork), temperance (humility, forgiveness), transcendence (gratitude, spirituality). These virtues are recognized and valued in almost every culture, and role models who embody these character strengths are honored. Parents seek to instill these virtues in their children. These are quintessential characteristics of the backstage. How do you prepare to move from your backstage to face the world? How do you wake up and engage the world? Do you leave your "dressing room" naked? Before going frontstage, consider clothing yourself in the six virtues. Remember your first meeting each day is a **_me_**eting with yourself. Ordering your backstage means being intentional about how you power up, reset, and power down each day.

Success is hard work
Success is heart work
Success is worth the work
So, do the work.

A Story Comes to Life

Truett Cathy's story shows us a Page Turner who successfully blends the backstage and the frontstage. You and I can thank him for the delicious chicken sandwiches and waffle fries available six days a week. Cathy is the founder of Chick-fil-A. I attended a distinguished event at the White House where Mr. Cathy and

Chick-fil-A were honored. Curious, I did a little research on Truett Cathy to discover what factors marked his backstage story, and what led to his frontstage success.

In reading his book, *Eat Mor Chikin—Doing Business the Chick-fil-A Way,* I learned of critical influences that shaped his backstage: the challenge of growing up during the Great Depression and feeling unloved by his dad. He also weathered the tragic loss of his two brothers in a plane crash and seeing his first restaurant burn to the ground. But he also had a mother who stressed the importance of faith as the cornerstone of life. Thus, in spite of family heartbreak and financial calamity, Cathy persisted. He kept turning the page in search of opportunities to fulfill his dream of owning a restaurant.

Today there are more than fifteen hundred Chick-fil-A restaurants. Two backstage values that seem directly connected to Cathy's life experiences govern Chick-fil-A: people and principles before profit and closed on Sundays. Their website explains:

"We should be about more than just selling chicken. We should be a part of our customers' lives and the communities in which we serve."

As part of this principle, Chick-fil-A provides college scholarships for restaurant team members, sponsors military appreciation events to support our troops, donates food to local shelters, and shows up at natural disasters to feed victims and first responders.

"For one day, our restaurants are still ... It's not about being closed. It's about how we use that time. So, while we're off today, we hope you can be with your family and friends. That's the thought behind each Sunday story—delivering recipes, activities, and inspiration that might bring you a little closer together."

Amazingly, Chick-fil-A generates more sales in six days than most fast food restaurants produce in seven. Page Turners like Truett Cathy don't just hang their values on the wall or post them on their website. They live them. They own them. Although they are clear that what they do (frontstage) is important, they realize that who they are (backstage) is more important.

The Point of the Story

- Frontstage is your public world of accomplishments, results, productivity, profit, and performance.

- Backstage is your private world of motives, values, virtues, purpose, and processing.

- Love and vulnerability shape your storyline.

- A nurtured backstage fosters frontstage success.

Your Developing Story

Take a moment for this brief one-minute exercise: Draw a picture of a tree.

When I give participants this exercise at my seminars, almost everyone draws the parts of the tree that are above-ground—trunk, branches, and leaves—very few people draw the roots. Interesting. When I ask why, they typically say, "Because you can't see them." That's exactly my point: We tend to ignore what we do not see; the roots are assumed and not drawn. Yet, they are the foundation of the tree. Likewise, we see the outgrowth of our backstage through the scenes of our story. As your heart and soul are nurtured (or not), so will the visible, frontstage aspects of your life follow suit.

1. In "The Happy Secret to Better Work" TED Talk, Dr. Shawn Achor explains that ten percent of long-term happiness is linked to external events and ninety percent

of long-term happiness lies in how the brain processes the world. According to Achor, when our brain is in a positive state, every single professional, personal, and educational outcome improves. Watch this TED Talk and challenge yourself to develop backstage happiness habits that resonate with your brain and can inspire you to be more productive on the frontstage.

2. Ready for this? Write your obituary. I know this sounds morbid, but the exercise is designed to bring into perspective what matters most. I can assure you no one will be reading your résumé at your funeral.

Chapter Three

Storylies vs. Storyline

"We become the stories we tell ourselves."

Elie Wiesel, Holocaust survivor

My sixth-grade teacher, Mrs. Stone, taught what was considered the top-tier math class and she meant well, I think. I suppose it was great I was placed in her class except I hated math and didn't want to compete with all the wanna-be Einsteins. Worse, Mrs. Stone's style was to send a group of students to the blackboard to solve math equations. I lived in abject terror of the day when my name would be called.

Then it happened. She called out, "Mintzer ... Moskowitz ... Parker." Our assignment was to reduce fractions. Mintzer and Moskowitz completed their assignments quickly, and I was left alone at the blackboard with thirty of my classmates staring a hole in my back. I scribbled numbers on the board, hoping the right combination might magically appear and rescue me from humiliation.

Apparently, Mrs. Stone grew impatient and said in front of everyone, "Johnny, you don't belong in this class." This wasn't the first time she had made such a comment, always in a tone of voice that sounded like a sneer.

What I heard her say that day was, "You're not good enough. You don't have what it takes. You can't cut it."

I made the mistake of believing Mrs. Stone. Her voice became the soundtrack of my life and leadership. For years, I was instantly angry whenever anyone questioned my competence. I lived with the fear of being "exposed" as a fraud. Only through prayer, journaling, and therapy did I begin to identify the "storylies" I believed. Storylie is a word I use to describe a destructive belief—a myth. It is the opposite of a storyline. As discussed earlier, the Page Turner storyline is composed of the five elements that create a better story: Demanding Bold Truth, Clarifying One's Quest, exhibiting Champion Generosity, Engaging Community, and Pursuing Continual Renewal. When we don't know or construct our own story, we allow others to hand us their script and feed us storylies. Then they, not we ourselves, define our story.

By going through my own counseling and heart work, I grieved, I wept, and I forgave Mrs. Stone. I never solved the math problem, but now understand her opinion was not the final word. I have resolved never again to allow anyone to write my story.

Have you ever felt limited because someone influential in your life didn't believe in you?

Have you ever found yourself thinking if so-and-so thinks that of me, it must be true?

Have you ever experienced the nagging suspicion that you're cruising through life living out an identity that isn't truly yours?

Perhaps these don't apply to you, but one day you came to the realization that, wow, you really could do or be more than your parents, teachers, boss, or coworkers ever thought possible!

Let's be honest. We are all susceptible to falling for storylies about our abilities and purpose, especially when the stories are told by people who matter most to us. Simply put, other people can wreak havoc with the authentic storyline that you were created to live.

Starting from when we are children, all the important people in our lives—parents, siblings, bosses, coworkers, pastors, teachers, coaches—play a huge role in shaping what we believe to be true about ourselves. And what we believe to be true is what we adopt as our life story. We see this in the movies. In *The Lord of the Rings* trilogy, Aragorn runs from his rightful position as king because he's afraid. He fears the character flaw of an ancestor and thinks it runs in his blood. That storylie sends him into self-exile, where he adopts the persona of a mysterious Ranger instead of donning the crown he was born to wear—just when Hobbits, Elf-kind, and humans really needed his leadership!

Refuse to Be Defined

Page Turners desire to do something big and meaningful with their lives. Regardless of whether they use the word dream, mission, vision, purpose, or calling, they want their lives to count for something significant. Without clarity about your mission in life, others take liberties, writing a version of your story they think you ought to be living. You become vulnerable to storylies. Don't let other people suck you into "storylies" they make up and maybe even believe about you.

This is not to say significant people in your life shouldn't influence your storyline. A Hebrew proverb says, "Plans fail for lack of counsel, but with many advisers, they succeed." Wisdom comes from seeking input and guidance from people we trust. They are often in a position to see things about ourselves we cannot. However, even the most trusted friends and advisors should not dictate our identity and purpose.

The Script I Nearly Gave My Son

My seventeen-year-old son, Joel, helped me understand the principle of storylies. Joel is an honor-roll student and at the time of this writing, is entering his senior year of high school. We have done our share of college tours, and we identified potential schools for his interest in marketing and business. During high school, he also started his own sneaker redesign and refurbishing business, taking used sneakers and repainting them. He saved his money and bought all the supplies: paint, brushes, and tape. He made business cards, and to this day he has customers paying thirty-five to forty dollars per pair.

Joel is also passionate about photography. He saved his money to buy a camera. Although he is an honor-roll student, something shifted for him. He began growing disillusioned with school. As he says, "I love learning, but I am uneasy with school." He's grown weary of studying required topics of no interest to him. He's now asking whether he can take a gap year and not go to college right away. He wants to take photography classes and attend a leadership program in Australia. That's a long way from home, and this plan has put my wife and me on edge.

Last summer, Joel attended a leadership program in Florida, and when he returned, he simply wanted to work his sneaker business and study photography. As his parents, this was a problem for us. We are supportive of his business, but we wanted him to have a steadier paycheck and experience a "real" work environment. Consequently, he applied to work in the local golf course clubhouse. He really wanted the job but didn't get it. He was willing to take a job, but only the jobs he wanted to work. Since he did not get the job he wanted, he wanted to focus on growing his business.

We discussed this several times. Finally, exasperated, I said to him, "You have not earned the right to decide which job you will work and which you won't." One morning while sitting on the deck drinking my morning smoothie, he came and sat with me and reminded me of my words, saying how much my words hurt him. I was aghast. I empathized with him, and I replied, "I understand what it feels like to want to do only what you are passionate about doing."

What's my point? I had a script in mind for Joel—to work a summer job, graduate high school, and go on to college. This was the script my wife and I followed. This was the script most kids follow. But Joel respectfully challenged the script. Let me be clear: it isn't that he is lazy or doesn't want to work or go to school. Joel loves earning money and learning. Yet a different story is stirring in his heart.

I realized I was handing Joel a script that wasn't consistent with his heart. I am learning as a dad that my son has a pencil and I have a pencil, and each life has its own page. In the writing of his story, I can only assist him. I asked Joel if he remembered the scene from The Pursuit of Happyness when Chris Gardner and his son are on the basketball court. Joel quoted the scene verbatim:

> **Christopher Gardner**: "Hey. Don't ever let somebody tell you ... you can't do something. Not even me. All right?"
>
> **Christopher**: "All right."
>
> **Christopher Gardner**: "You got a dream. You gotta protect it. People can't do somethin' themselves, they wanna tell you you can't do it. If you want somethin', go get it. Period."

I may not always agree with my son, but I trust his judgment, integrity, and heart. And I don't want to foist my script for his life onto him. He must develop the script for his own life, while I am here to guide and encourage.

Scripts Others Give You

After his first audition, actor Sidney Poitier heard these potentially debilitating words from a casting director: "Why don't you stop wasting people's time and go out and become a dishwasher or something?" At that moment, recalls Poitier, he decided to devote his life to acting. He refused to let someone else decide his life path.

Young Michael Jordan was cut from his high school basketball team because of his "lack of skill." Yet he rejected the storylie spelled out for him by a visionless coach and went on to become an NBA superstar.

When Albert Einstein was in school, his grades were so poor his parents thought he was mentally retarded, and a teacher told him, "You will never amount to anything!" He refused to let those storylies define him, going on to become a theoretical physicist of such renown that today his name is practically synonymous with "genius."

My friend Dr. Jay Strack had the rare privilege of accompanying the family of Dr. Martin Luther King Jr. when some of his archives were opened for the first time. In one of the many wow moments of the day, Coretta Scott King opened one of Dr. King's college report cards and said, "So this is obviously before he was Dr. King!" To everyone's amazement, Dr. King's lowest grade was in communication. In the comments section of the report card, the professor had written, "Martin, if you continue to use that flowery language, no one will ever listen to you."

Aren't you glad Dr. King did not follow the script his professor handed to him? In fiction and in real life, we see people who wrote new narratives for themselves in time to recognize their callings, embrace their purposes and—in the process—make the world a better place. What are you waiting for?

Part of the work of embracing your true calling and purpose is identifying the storylies you've come to believe. Let's look at a few of the common storylies that cause people to live well below their potential. Do any of these sound familiar?

The More Storylie: "More is better."

Do you live your life wanting more? More experiences? More things? More options? More money? Here's the question: Why? How will your life be different if you got more?

This storylie is compelling in our day and age. In fact, according to Peter Drucker, "In a few hundred years ... it is likely that the most important event historians will see is not technology, not the Internet, not e-commerce. For the first time—literally—substantial and rapidly growing numbers of people have choices. For the first time, they will have to manage themselves. And society is totally unprepared for it."

Part of what makes the "more is better" storylie so oppressive is deciding among the myriad options on the journey to "more, more, and more." The truth is, managing all the options and increase can be exhausting. In fact, psychologists have a name for it: decision fatigue.

If you've bought into this storylie, the fatigue and distractions can be enormous. You might think that having more is empowering, or a sign that you are on the right path. The bottom line is that the perennial quest for more is debilitating and overwhelming. In the end, this storylie will, ironically, leave you with far fewer resources to live the life you want.

The Busy Storylie: "The more I do, the more significant I am."

Somehow, busyness has become a badge of honor to many in our society. Be careful of racing toward a finish line that doesn't exist. I must confess that there was a time in my life when I enjoyed hearing people say, "Dr. Parker, I know you're a very busy person, but I was wondering if ..." Truth be told, I liked being

41

considered special and important. Being too busy meant I was in demand, needed, and relied upon. Or so I thought. Maybe being too busy just meant I unwisely took on too many responsibilities and failed to maintain boundaries by using the word "no."

Now, I despise the idea of people perceiving me as too busy even to approach. I do not want busyness to define my relationships or to define me. I don't want to live that story. According to Wayne Muller, author of Legacy of the Heart, the Chinese word for "busy" is composed of two characters: "killing" and "heart." What a profound image of the consequences of constant busyness in our lives. I would go a step further and say persistent busyness is a killer of our calling, purpose, and dreams as well.

Have you bought into the storylie that the busier you are, the more important you are? Or perhaps you keep yourself busy, not to muster a sense of importance, but to hide from emotional pain. Henri Nouwen, the well-renowned writer and priest, once wrote: "... we panic when there is nothing or nobody left to distract us. When we have no project to finish, no friend to visit, no book to read, no television to watch or no record to play, and when we are left all alone by ourselves, we are brought so close to the revelation of our basic human aloneness ... we will do anything to get busy again and continue the game which makes us believe that everything is fine after all." I hope you will come to look at your calendar as an ally rather than an adversary. Don't be victimized by our time-crunch society, where everyone is hurried and harried. You control each minute of each day. And when you do, each moment can be rich and rewarding. Be careful of mistaking busyness for significance."

The Shame Storylie: "I am not enough."

Mike was someone working with me on a seminar project. I called him to check on his progress with a particular aspect of the work. Let me explain that finding anyone more talented than Mike is extremely difficult. On the phone that day, he said he had not sent me his portion of the project because it wasn't perfect. He went on to say he feared my criticism, which he felt as rejection—he wanted to keep on working until his portion was perfect.

Mike and I grew up together, and I had never heard him reveal himself in this way. I was shocked since I had envied him when we were younger due to his exceptional talents. He knew early in his story what he was going to do with his life. His abilities even earned him a scholarship to college. Although Mike was profoundly gifted, shame gripped his heart and affected how he saw himself.

Guilt says, "I made a mistake." Shame says, "I am a mistake." How we see ourselves affects the story we write. As Mike's admission shows, at its core, shame is rooted in fear. How do we get to the place of accepting our imperfections? The fact Mike could be this honest meant he was still in the wrestling match and had not thrown in the towel in submission to shame. Winning the battle over shame is indeed a daily fight. To be vulnerable and admit your struggle as Mike did takes courage and strength.

I appreciate the great work Brené Brown has done in researching shame. Read her book *Daring Greatly,* where she advises us how to be resilient when the "gremlins" of shame surface.

The Isolation Storylie: "To admit I need help is a sign of weakness."

This is the Lone Ranger mentality—buying into western culture's ideals of individualism and self-reliance. The person who embraces this lie will typically say "I'm good" when you ask,

"How are you doing?" or "Do you need any help?" no matter what is really happening,

In the 1970s, the musical duo Simon and Garfunkel had a popular song, "I Am a Rock," which spoke to the temptation to isolate and try to be sufficient without others. Just like there are laws of physics in the universe, there are laws for healthy living. This "I am a rock" lie violates relational laws. We are unable to fulfill our mission and reach our destiny alone. To confront the isolation storylie, remember this: isolation kills, connection heals, collaboration builds.

The Validation Storylie: "Approval from you will make me okay."

During her acceptance speech, while receiving an Academy Award for the film Places in the Heart, actress Sally Fields said, "I can't deny the fact that you like me. Right now, you like me!" She was in joyful disbelief at winning. But I have wondered, were these words seeking validation? I am not criticizing Sally Fields for I have wrestled with this lie of seeking approval and living in fear of being rejected by people.

You post a thought via social media that no one "likes" except your mother. What does this do to you? I coach clients who feel discouraged because they get a weak response to their social media postings compared to others. They compare and despair. This naturally leads to my questions, "Why are you posting? What do you want to get out of it? What do you want to hear back?"

We have been created with a thirst for love, relationship, and purpose. Beware! If we allow ourselves to become too thirsty, we will drink anything. Becoming too thirsty is chasing validation. It's an exhausting and dangerous desert we enter when we base our worth, security, and legitimacy on what other people think of us. We may rely on important people in our lives—parents, spouse, friends, boss—to define us. Or we may try to conform to abstract ideas and cultural archetypes, e.g., "the beauty queen," "the man of iron," and cultural expectations we feel we must live up to. Unless we learn our way out of this trap, we'll keep drinking what is essentially seawater, chasing validation that only makes us thirstier.

The Happy Storylie: "I will be happy when . . ."

"When I get married, then I'll be happy."
"When I get out of this marriage, then I'll be happy."
"When I get a job, then I'll be happy."
"When I get the next job, then I'll be happy."
"When I move to a better neighborhood, then I'll be happy."

You see the pattern? There's always another "when." There are variations, of course. For some, the phrase they've bought into might sound more like, "If only [fill in the blank], then [fill in the blank]." If only I had more money, then I could make a difference in the world. If only I had more time, then I could pursue my dreams. If only I had more education (or a nicer spouse, or a bigger paycheck, or a more extroverted personality), then I could be the person I've always wanted to be." Now is the time to stop living for that "someday" that will magically make your life come together.

I've always loved this quote from philosopher Alfred D'Souza: "For a long time, it had seemed to me that life was about to begin—real life. But there was always some obstacle in the way. Something to be got through first, some unfinished business, time still to be served, a debt to be paid, then life would begin. At last, it dawned on me that these obstacles were my life."

What a freeing thought! You don't have to wait another minute. You're already doing it —you're living your life. So be intentional and make your life count.

The Social Media Storylie: "I experience close relationships and achieve fulfillment through technology."

How many times have you checked your email today? Scrolled through Facebook? Sent or received a text? Sat down at your computer to get some work done and found yourself distracted by a blog, video, or website that, while interesting, is completely unrelated to anything you need to get done that day?

Relentless distractions have become a modern-day plague. Visual clutter, information overload, digital distractions, and opinion drama are everywhere we turn. In fact, the pull of digital distractions is so great that you don't even have to be holding your cell phone to be essentially absent from your life and relationships. Researchers from the University of Essex found that people who engaged in personal discussions when their cell phones were nearby and in view reported lower relationship quality and decreased feelings of trust.

Social media "distance" is such a problem that there are movements to encourage folks to disconnect from the virtual Matrix that permeates our lives. Every March, the nonprofit organization Reboot inspires thousands of people to unplug from their devices for at least twenty-four hours. Google, for example, is leading a new trend of offering courses for employees that encourage mindfulness and digital detoxing in the workplace. Camp Grounded is a "digital detox camp" that offers hyper-connected attendees a respite from the incessant noise of Facebook, Twitter, and the avalanche of other media relentlessly battling for their attention.

Do you think you are just a little bit cooler when you are plugged in? Are you using the clutter of technology to distract you from pain, doubts, or fears? Did you start because technology offered conveniences, but now you're more hooked than you'd like to admit?

Technology and social media were designed to be tools for communicating. They were not intended to become our life and replace relationships. Many of my clients are restless and unable to sleep without having the TV on or having their cell phone nearby. Let's be honest. We can use the noise of social media to drown pain and to live vicariously through someone else's story. Or we can present a false or idealized story to a distant audience. Without the routines of social media, moments of silence and solitude mean confronting our true aloneness and our need for more personal and authentic communication.

The Identity Storylie: "My image is who I am."

Has there ever been such a time in the history of the world when "image" was so easy to create? Or held such a prominent place in our priorities? Don't confuse identity with identifiers. Your career, appearance, ethnicity, and possessions are all examples of identifiers. Also, do not mistake identity for image. Your identity is based on your character.

Our current "culture of image" is a fairly recent development. Throughout the eighteenth century, people were more concerned with private behavior. There was, according to historian Warren Susman, a "culture of character." In fact, writings of the day reflected the nation's focus on character, exploring concepts such as duty, discipline, work, service, reputation, morals, and honor.

The shift to a preoccupation with image built momentum in the early nineteenth century. For the first time, the Industrial Revolution created opportunities to work next to people who weren't relatives or neighbors, and people began figuring out how to make a good impression on others. In this new environment, it was important to ramp up quickly, to look for clues about new coworkers, and to find ways to communicate how you wanted to be perceived. Once again, writings of the day reflected society's interests, but now words like sparkling, magnetic, and attractive filled advice books and columns. In the twentieth century, our appetite for "image" advice continued to grow, and we saw both men and women striving to learn how to "dress for success."

Don't buy into the storylie that what you look like on the outside (frontstage)—or even the impressions you create through social media—carry more weight than who you are on the inside (backstage). We may no longer live in a culture of character, but that doesn't mean your character isn't one of the most important facets of who you are.

Therefore, take ownership and responsibility for the stories you believe about yourself. Decide if these storylies apply to you; if not, they will take root and will leave you a frenzied and scattered soul. And that kind of soul yields a frenzied and scattered life.

A Story Comes to Life

In the movie, *The Truman Show,* Jim Carey plays Truman Burbank, the star of an unusual reality TV show. He's not just in the show, he is the show. Cameras began rolling the day Truman was born. For nearly thirty years, viewers watched every moment of his life—his first steps, his first girlfriend, and his first job.

Truman lives in Seahaven, an elaborate film set inside a giant Hollywood studio. His hometown is on an island and comes complete with fake sun and moon, its own weather, and a "citizenry" of extras. Everything about his life is carefully scripted, controlled and completely phony. The problem is, Truman doesn't know it. The show's producer, Cristof, works hard to keep it that way.

Slowly, Truman starts to suspect his world is not all it seems to be. A studio light crashes in the street, and news reports say it fell off an airplane. When he inadvertently sees the show's production crew at work, his "wife" passes it off as a freak accident. Truman tries to leave Seahaven but can't get a flight for a month. Then a nuclear reactor accident closes the only road out of town.

Truman can't explain, but he knows there must be more to life than what he's experienced so far. In desperation, he defies his fear of water and sails off the island. Christof orchestrates a hurricane and nearly drowns him, but it's no use. In the end, Truman reaches the horizon—actually, the studio wall—and enters the real world. When he finds the exit from his make-believe life, he sheds his pretend, image-managed self and discovers who he really is.

Truman has a lot to teach us. All his life, he was unaware his identity was imaginary. He never suspected he could be more than the role he played. He lived in a world of distractions and distortions—storylies. This is how most people live in our real world. Our misperceptions and empty pursuits form phony horizons that separate us from a deeper reality. Turning the page—embracing our unique calling—enables us to realize we are not the roles we have played. We will understand that we're not constructed of other people's expectations.

The Point of the Story

- Refuse to allow others to define your story

- A storylie is a myth you have believed

- Recognize the storylies you have believed

Your Developing Story

In your search for a life that's real, assess where you are. The wheel of life diagram has eight sections representing various areas of your life. The exercise measures your level of satisfaction in these areas. With zero at the center and ten at the outer edge (the ideal), rank your level of satisfaction with each life arena by circling where you are on the wheel. Have any storylies applied to these arenas in the past?

Wheel of Life

NAME: _____   **DATE:** _____

Faith   Firm (Career)

Fun and
Recreation   Finances

0   10

Future and
Planning   Fitness

Friends   Family

WHEEL OF LIFE INSTRUCTIONS
The 8 sections in the Wheel of Life represent intentionality.

- Please change, split or rename any category so that it's meaningful and represents a life of intentionality.
- Next, taking the centre of the wheel as 0 and the outer edge as 10, rank your **level of satisfaction** with each area out of 10 by drawing a straight or curved line to create a new outer edge (see example)
- The new perimeter of the circle represents **your** 'Wheel of Life'. Is it a bumpy ride?

EXAMPLE

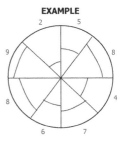

ACT I

Dream: Know Your Story

"Once upon a time…"

Many people have lost sight of their dream—if they ever had one. For someone to have a grand adventure, they must first have a big dream. Turning the page to an exhilarating future begins with nurturing and naming one's dream, which emanates from your soul. It's said that Martin Luther King's "I Have a Dream" was not the speech he planned to give that day. His speechwriters had helped craft a different speech. But gospel singer Mahalia Jackson was on the platform, and after Dr. King had spoken just a few sentences of his prepared speech, she began saying, "Tell 'em about the dream, Martin!" The story goes, Dr. King pushed his notes aside and began speaking extemporaneously from his soul. Thus was born one of the greatest speeches—and inspiration to dream big. To dream big involves Demanding Bold Truth and Clarifying Ones' Quest.

Chapter Four

Demand Bold Truth

"Better a cruel truth than a
comfortable delusion."

Edward Abbey

Breaking Story: Humility Before Honor

When it comes to turning the page in your life and taking a big leap forward, there is a secret ingredient many people overlook: humility. This concept is widely misunderstood, as many people equate humility with being compliant, subservient, submissive, and even passive. Some think humble people are pushovers or doormats. This is utter nonsense and completely misses the point.

True humility comes from a place of strength, not weakness. Humble men and women have an inner core that lets them serve others and put others first. They have the courage to take personal responsibility for their actions—including their failures—without blaming others. They are more interested in hearing someone else's story than trying to impress people with their own story.

In his book *Aspire*, Kevin Hall explores the etymology of powerful words. He explains, "The origin of the word humility is the Latin word 'humus' meaning soil, specifically rich, dark and organic. When a seed is planted in fertile soil, it transforms into something far greater." According to Hall, "When we have sufficient humus in our lives, we grow and develop, and help those around us to flourish."

Not surprisingly, the empirical research on humility shows that this trait has great value. Humility has been linked with better academic performance, job performance, and excellence in leadership. Humble people have better social relationships, avoid deception in their social interactions, and tend to be forgiving, grateful, and cooperative.

Remember earlier when I said that humility is a secret ingredient? Let me amend that to say humility is the key ingredient to success and Demanding Bold Truth. Humility is essential for all who wish to turn the page and move toward a richer, more meaningful life.

People seek me out for coaching when they are languishing, not flourishing. Less than twenty percent of Americans feel their lives are flourishing. By flourishing, I am referring to a sense of wellness and purpose—spiritually, physically, emotionally and in relationships (Keyes, C.). They feel stuck in a bad story and want to write a different one. I listen, empathize, and affirm their reality. I tell them "Yes, you are stuck in a bad story, but there's good news. You can turn the page. You can write a different and better story."

Writing a different story requires a magical, eight-letter word—humility, facing the truth about yourself, and about circumstances. Go to YouTube and listen to the lyrics of Michael Jackson's "Man in the Mirror"—the national anthem of humility.

A Look in the Mirror

Every Wednesday I have a five a.m. phone conversation with my friend, Chris. We are committed to having a meaningful conversation about our lives and our stories every week.

"We write our stories based on those who taught us to write," Chris said one morning. What a true statement! None of us had a choice in how our stories began. And if our stories aren't turning out the way we hoped, we easily can blame those who guided the pen as our lives took shape. But at some point, we must accept responsibility for writing our own stories and deciding how the rest will go.

You see the process in countless movies and books. All protagonists experience something that requires a long, hard look in the mirror. Once Jake Scully discovers the government plans to take the people's land in Avatar, will he live in denial? Or will he let the ugly truth inspire him to turn a page and embrace a nobler mission?

We must have the courage to look inside, demand truth, and then act boldly on that truth. That means owning our shortcomings and strengths fearlessly, admitting the truth to ourselves and to those who have earned the right to hear our stories.

From Pain to Purpose

I am convinced our life purpose or raison d'etre can become clearer through pain. This happens only if we choose to make room for pain and allow pain to mentor us. Yes, pain hurts. And, like you, I don't like to suffer. Yet, none of us are immune. The rain of pain falls in every life, and I can't deny I've grown more from my pains and failures than from my successes. Pain has functioned as a cleansing agent and served to introduce me to my true self. The chapters of pain we experience can suck the hope and ambition out of us. We experience loss, disappointment, grief, and bitterness. Here is where we may easily get stuck. We tell ourselves stories about pain—usually not to understand the messages of our pain but to blame life for allowing us to suffer. Permitting yourself to get stuck in a chapter of pain may make you feel justified in unhealthy "painkillers." That is, we overuse prescribed medications, we look to escape through common vices like sex, illegal drugs, or anything else we rely on to numb our pain.

Remember the story I shared earlier about being downsized from my dream consulting job? I felt angry and rejected. But as I began Demanding Bold Truth of myself, pain awakened me to my true self (backstage). Pain exposed my motives and how I had been using my work to define my worth; I identified the real reason for my pain. Pain has a way of waking us up to our true calling.

In *It's a Wonderful Life*, George Bailey dreams of leaving Bedford Falls, attending college, traveling to Europe, and becoming an architect. But when his dad dies, George reluctantly assumes ownership of the faltering family business. When George is on the brink of financial ruin and contemplating suicide, wishing he had never been born, Clarence, the guardian angel, gives George his wish. Through this experience, George realizes the essence of his life is in relationships, and he is able to appreciate his impact on family and community as his purpose.

Often Page Turners start with one desire but must face adversity before their real purpose manifests. In *Hunger Games*, Katniss is a hunter from the poor mining town of District 12. Her life is interrupted when she volunteers to take her sister's place in the country's annual televised death match; saving her sister's life was her first goal. However, after Katniss wins despite grueling trials, she returns home and begins a quiet revolution against the tyrannical government. We discover deeper purpose only through Demanding Bold Truth of ourselves. And demanding truth takes a supporting cast, pain, and the time to process our discoveries to gain a sense of our story. To unveil your better story, you first must bury the old story.

Demanding Bold Truth:

- Requires the very best of you

- Means being imperfect but being humble and perfectly honest when falling short

- Takes courage to compassionately hold people responsible for their best

- Takes courage to settle for nothing less than the genuine

- Takes courage to say "no" and allow room for people's disappointment

- Means fearlessly not apologizing for who you are becoming

- Means not trying to be 'the man' or 'the diva'—just the best you can be

- Means being brave enough to become the person deserving of your dream

Demanding Bold Truth as a Leader

I want to share what I wrote to the executive team of an organization I lead. After some sincere soul searching, I had come to some unpleasant realizations. To embrace authenticity and take action, I shared the truth about my new commitments with those who had been working closely with me.

Dear Team,

I am clear about my strengths, gifts, and what I do well. But I have ignored areas of immaturity. I am convinced that healthy leadership emanates from the soul of the leader. And if that soul is unhealthy, everything and everyone is affected.

So how have I been immature? Too often I have used the organization as a validation of my success. I have avoided difficult conversations because I am uneasy with conflict. I have cared far too much about what people think of me. I have operated in pride, not asking for help ("I'm supposed to be Dr. Parker with a doctorate in leadership") yet I struggle with delegating and thinking strategically. I refuse to allow this foolish and immature thinking to linger in my life.

For these reasons, I have been seeing a counselor/coach twice a month to help me to grow emotionally and in relationships. I have also resumed meeting with other leaders who discuss their leadership challenges and hold each other accountable for growth. I have shared my shortcomings as a leader and asked for their help.

I am extremely optimistic about the future of our organization and am more committed than ever to seeing men become dynamic leaders in all that they do.

Sincerely,

Dr. J

This kind of direct acknowledgment helped the group to see me as someone growing too and dedicated enough to the needs of the group to address my shortcomings. Sharing the letter helped group members explore their own issues, strengthening the group as we faced truths together.

Demanding Bold Truth As a CEO

I happened to be in a Starbucks when the staff began shutting down at five p.m. Thus, I had personal experience of a courageous example of Demanding Bold Truth. In 2008, Starbucks CEO Howard Schultz faced rapidly falling stock values, flagging sales, growing customer dissatisfaction, and other challenges. He summoned two hundred senior leaders to corporate headquarters in Seattle to address what he called "the erosion of Starbucks' soul."

In his book, *Onward*, Schulz writes: "We looked in the mirror, and we said, 'Ladies and gentlemen, let's be honest with one another. We are not doing this as well as we once did, and the mediocrity that we have been embracing cannot stand any longer.'"

After Demanding Bold Truth from himself and others at the corporate level, Schultz bravely asked seven thousand stores to close early one day so employees could receive additional training. Closing early was unprecedented for a retail chain that would voluntarily lose millions of dollars. Schultz said, "This was a moment that required honesty about our situation as well as sincere optimism that we would get through it."

Schultz could have chosen to let the business continue down its path, ignoring the truth and passing blame. But he had the courage to face facts and devise strategies to address them.

Demanding Bold Truth in Sports

I applaud Urban Meyer for Demanding Bold Truth when anxiety consumed him, and perfectionism was killing him. His life's story had become a mystery to himself. So, Meyer quit his dream job as University of Florida football coach—leaving $20 million on the table—for a hiatus from the sport and one-on-one time with his soul.

In the months away from the game he loved, Meyer seriously examined his life and the story his life was telling versus the story he wanted it to tell. He asked soul-centric questions such as Why am I doing this? Why do I coach? How can I be a good dad and husband and still have career success?

Based on the truth he embraced in finding the answers to these questions, he took decisive actions. Today, a contract signed with his family hangs on the wall behind his desk, a direct result of Coach Meyer taking ownership of his weaknesses, strengths, choices, and life:

- My family will always come first.

- I will take care of myself and maintain good health.

- I will go on a trip once a year—minimum—with Nicki (his daughter).

- I will not go more than nine hours a day at the office.

- I will sleep with my cellphone on silent.

- I will continue to communicate daily with my kids.

- I will trust God's plan and not be overanxious.

- I will keep the lake house.

- I will find a way to watch Nicki and Gigi play volleyball.

- I will eat three meals a day.

Urban Meyer was intentional about demanding truth and acting on that truth. As a result, he turned the page in his story and returned to coaching with a better resolve.

Demanding Bold Truth About Prejudice

In 2006, a man was shot and killed by NYPD on the morning of his wedding day. His name was Sean Bell, and he was my younger cousin. His death gave me a front-row seat to pain, grief, confusion, and anger.

What I know for sure is—whether we're talking about my cousin Sean; Mike Brown in Ferguson, Missouri; Eric Garner at Staten Island; the police in general; or the criminal justice system—we can't address prejudice without Demanding Bold Truth. Taking personal responsibility for one's behavior takes courage. Playing the blame game only creates defensiveness in others. We all have a story and desire that it be heard. What would happen if we dared to sit courageously across from our adversaries not only to share our story but to hear theirs?

What do we as African-Americans wish the police, the judicial system, or America could hear about our story? What do police and the judicial system wish African-Americans would hear about their own stories as well? We can't turn the page without the humility and bravery to hear and empathize with the other, whoever that "other" is.

I have been married twenty-seven years. My wife and I battled feelings of frustration early in our marriage when we didn't feel heard or respected by each other. We were uncomfortable with our differences, which led to friction. Instead of looking directly at our differences and doing the work necessary to understand them, I felt tempted to strike out physically when my wife criticized me. In general, when people don't appropriately process the pain and discomfort of their differences, they are prone to act in destructive ways. In marriages, this can lead to affairs and domestic violence; when confronting cultural and racial differences, the result is stereotypes, prejudice, and injustice on both sides.

Being hurt and angry doesn't give anyone the right to hurt others. The wisdom of Dr. King is helpful: "An eye for an eye leaves everyone blind." I thank God I never acted on the emotions that would lead to domestic violence with my wife. I sought counseling, determined to work through my emotional injury and to be a healthy man at any cost. Admitting I was wounded and seeking help stands out as one of my most courageous acts.

Prejudice is rooted in the fear of difference. We typically don't embrace difference germane to politics, gender, religion, or race. Instead, our human tendency is to fear and criticize difference, to seek to control difference or try to change those different from ourselves.

My wife and I remain very different, but through emotional sweat and tears, we've learned to celebrate our differences. Personal ownership and vulnerability can create an atmosphere where healthy change is possible. What would happen if everyone learned to overcome the discomfort of differences and to appreciate and celebrate them, just as we learn to first taste and then love different cuisines? When young, we only tolerate plain noodles with butter, but as we grow, we gradually learn to expand our tastes and savor foreign foods—the spicy, the crunchy, the bitter, and the sweet and sour. Strong relationships are built through vulnerability, experimentation, and trust, which demands bold truth.

Radio personality Dr. David Anderson said, "Distance demonizes. It's hard to hate up close." The good news is that "up-close" relationships are slowly starting to be built. Pastor Tony Lee of the Community of Hope AME Church in Hillcrest Heights, Maryland, recently invited the local police chief to address the church and share his heart. At the University of Maryland, students and campus police periodically play pickup basketball games in an effort to know each other better.

It requires grit to own our motives and fears, to do our work of the heart. The heart of the matter is a matter of the heart. We must interview our hearts with questions such as:

- What am I pretending not to see?

- What do you want me to hear that I am not hearing?

- Where do I need to accept responsibility fearlessly?

- Do I treat others the way I want to be treated?

I watched my cousin Valerie, Sean's mother, do her heart work. Instead of blaming other people and the police, she has demanded bold truth to grieve and exchange bitterness for forgiveness. She has empathized with other mothers who suffered the loss of sons. She speaks at events, protests respectfully, and has written a book honoring Sean's life. Her hope has been in God's ability to bring beauty from ashes. She refuses to allow her pain to be wasted. Through her pain, her purpose has become magnified.

Turning the Page by Owning Our Strengths

Demanding Bold Truth isn't just about owning our shortcomings or challenges but also includes owning our strengths. Many of us strive to improve, yet we focus on our failings instead of the parts that are strong and flourishing. I appreciate this quote from Marianne Williamson, who says:

Our deepest fear is not that we are inadequate. Our deepest fear is that we are powerful beyond measure. It is our light, not our darkness, that most frightens us. We ask ourselves, who am

I to be brilliant, gorgeous, talented, and fabulous? Actually, who are you not to be? You are a child of God. Your playing small doesn't serve the world. There's nothing enlightened about shrinking so that other people won't feel insecure around you.

Does telling yourself the truth about your strengths make you uncomfortable? If you acknowledge the things you're truly good at, won't you have to confront the insecurities that keep you from operating daily in your strengths? Martin Seligman and other researchers in the field of positive psychology have found we are happier and less depressed when engaged in work that uses our strengths in new and innovative ways.

A Work of ART

Demanding Bold Truth is a work of ART.

- A = Being authentic

  Who am I?

- R = Being relational

  Who are the people that love me and are willing to tell me the truth?

- T = Being transparent

  What do I need to stop, start, or continue doing?

When we neglect our ART work, we succumb to living artificially. According to Roman folk history, dishonest stone sculptors hid flaws in their work by filling them with wax. Eventually, the wax melted, and the sculptor's poor work was exposed. Honest sculptors stamped their work with "sine cere," which is Latin for "without wax."

Demanding Bold Truth is a journey, not a destination, striving to live authentically—without wax. *Authentic leaders, according to* Harvard business professor Bill George, are people who own their mistakes, acknowledge their faults, and seek to put their organizations' interests ahead of their own.

Demanding Bold Truth can be uncomfortable, because we may fear admitting our flaws smacks of "failure." But it's also daunting because, deep down, we know it's the path to claiming our strengths and successes, which some of us fear even more. You don't have to Demand Bold Truth from yourself. But when authentic truth is lacking, you must deal with the consequences.

When we are faced with the need for change, a solution, or progress, nothing happens unless we look squarely in the mirror and speak the truth to ourselves. Unless we turn the page, we will continue on the same path, writing the same unsatisfying story, stuck in the same limitations we've grown to hate. We'll deflect our challenges and devalue our strengths, remaining stuck in pain, mediocrity, and blame shifting.

If the leader of a company, ministry, community or family sticks his head in the sand and doesn't search for the critical truths of his actions and his mission, everyone they hope to lead will suffer, too. Demanding Bold Truth, on the other hand, fosters physical, emotional, relational, and spiritual health. It promotes vitality, change, and freedom. Demanding Bold Truth is the road less traveled but a road worth traveling. It is the only way to become real and flourish.

A Story Comes to Life

In the movie, *Flight*, Whip Whitaker (Denzel Washington) is a seasoned pilot who encounters a mid-air catastrophe, yet he is able to fly and land the plane with nearly every passenger surviving. Initially, he is applauded for this feat. But, when the National Transportation Safety Board examined what happened and performed a drug test on Whip—the results showed he was intoxicated during the flight. Whip's friend Charlie secures an attorney who tries to get the toxicology report dismissed to save Whip's career and prevent him from going to jail. Clearly, Whip's defense team is more invested in Whip's success than he is, because he continues to drink and use cocaine. A turn the page moment is when Whip is being commended in court for successfully landing the plane, but is questioned regarding the two empty vodka bottles in the plane's garbage. The only other person who tested positive was Trina, the deceased flight attendant. Whip could have lied and blamed Trina, but he demands bold truth of himself and confesses he is an addict. The scene shifts to Whip in jail telling his story to other inmates. His confession lost him his family and his license; he can never pilot a plane again. Yet, he acknowledges how grateful he is to be sober and free. In the final scene, Whip's son visits him to discuss a college application essay on "the most fascinating person that I've never met." Sitting across from his dad, Whip's son begins by asking him, "Who are you?" The movie ends with a plane flying above and Whip's reply, "That's a good question."

Whip Whitaker's story reminds me of my parents' real-life story. After nine years of marriage, they had experienced all the challenges every marriage faces—family baggage, communication, and conflict. Then they divorced. For many years, they went their separate ways. But as time went on, they began to Demand Bold Truth. They stopped blaming each other and started owning their respective roles in their marital story. They humbled themselves. They apologized and forgave each other. After they had been divorced for thirty-six years, I had the privilege of remarrying them. Today, having learned to take ownership of their challenges keeps them from getting stuck in the blame game. Discovering their strengths lets them serve joyfully at their church and open their home and share their story with the young couples in their neighborhood. They are experiencing a new love story because they embraced humility and demanded bold truth.

Point of the Story

- Humility before honor

- Demanding Bold Truth is fearlessly owning your challenges

- Demanding Bold Truth is fearlessly owning your strengths

Developing Story—For Demanding Bold Truth

The "Born" Identity

The "Born" Identity Tool helps you explore your life in ten-year intervals—defining scenes, emotional themes, and the title of the story for each decade. When using this tool, my clients almost always see their personal patterns of strength and challenge and receive clues about their life's calling. By carefully reviewing their history, they gain clarity about their future. Use a large sheet of paper, put it on a wall and review your life timeline. Don't be surprised if this exercise produces tears.

1.   **Letter Therapy**

These three letters will spur your growth. Choose the letter you most need to write at this time in your life.

A. **THE FEAR LETTER**

Write a letter to fear as if you were writing to a person. Describe how fear has held you hostage and explain your determination not to let it rule you.

B. **THE FORTITUDE LETTER**

Similar to the fear letter, write a letter to fortitude describing your strengths, how you refuse to apologize for them, and how you will develop your strengths to serve the world.

C. **THE FORGIVENESS LETTER**

Sometimes the truth involves an admission we have been unwilling to make—before we can turn the page in our stories, there is someone we need to forgive. Failing to forgive harms us in many ways, with perhaps the greatest being that it anchors us to an old story, making it virtually impossible to move on, move freely, and move confidently in a new direction.

I encourage you to try it. Writing a letter to the person who caused you emotional injury can be indescribably powerful. Describe your hurt and any other emotions you have regarding the event—don't hold back! Close your letter by adding a statement of forgiveness, such as "Even though you never asked me, I choose to forgive you."

Moreover, it is possible that, before we can turn the page, we need to request forgiveness for emotional injury we caused someone else. Just as bitterness can anchor us to old stories, so can guilt and shame. Note that these letters are not meant to be given to the person you wounded or the one who wounded you. The letters are for you, to flush out what's been stored in the bottom of your heart.

2. **Seek Outside Insight**

We live our lives on a stage, allowing most people to see the choreographed play while inviting very few behind the curtains where life is messy. And yet if we have hopes of abandoning denial, blame, and victimhood in exchange for the power to change our stories, we would do well to give trusted people access to our backstage. Working with a life coach, mentor, or counselor can be invaluable.

3. **Take the Virtues in Action Strengths Survey** at www.viacharacter.org.

This free online survey describes twenty-four virtues and strengths and takes about twenty minutes to complete.

4. **See the Clifton Strengths Finder by Gallup**

Examine this tool for a thorough assessment of your strengths at www.gallupstrengthscenter.com. Their research shows people who use their strengths every day are six times more likely to be fully engaged at work.

Chapter Five

Clarify Your Quest

"Get busy living or get busy dying."

Andy, *Shawshank Redemption*

Breaking Story: Stillness Before Strategy

Business gurus and motivational speakers often tell us to begin a new venture by creating a "mission statement" or "business plan." But there is a critical step that must come before—reflecting, pondering, praying, and seeking the guidance that will decide how your life story will play out. Determining who we are and what we want to do with our lives begins by soul searching, taking inventory, assessing our passions, and accessing wise guidance. We must press "pause" on our busy lives long enough to evaluate if we're moving in the direction we truly want to go. The Trappist monk Thomas Merton affirmed this idea when he said, "Not all men are called to be hermits, but all men need enough silence and solitude in their lives to enable the deep inner voice to be heard at least occasionally."

I've worked with hundreds of people who felt stuck in a bad story. Though these men and women generally worked hard doing good things, they had a nagging sense that they were missing out on something. Indeed, many people struggle with the questions, "What am I really here for? What's my unique purpose and calling?" They want to do something meaningful and significant with their lives ... but what?

This points to the importance of setting aside time for stillness and solitude. Think of it this way: With a clear plastic cup, I took water from the Chesapeake Bay. I allowed it to sit for several minutes and slowly the particles from the bay settled in the bottom of the cup and the water became clearer at the top. Similarly, setting aside time for stillness to contemplate can lead to clarity and point the way to the life we want. Creating space in your life to explore and dream enables you to contemplate your unique contribution to the world. When you tune out all the voices around you screaming for attention, you can listen to your life.

When I talk to people about turning the page in their lives, they are usually so eager to get moving in a new direction that they blow past the most important step: thoughtfully and intentionally listening for wise guidance and listening to their soul. Times of deep reflection enable you to clearly identify your desires, explore your motivations, and ensure that the next chapters of your story are exactly what you want them to be.

One of my favorite cartoons shows Lucy sitting at her five-cent psychology booth, where Charlie Brown has stopped for advice about life. Lucy explains, "Life is like a deck chair. On the cruise ship of life, some people place their chair at the rear of the ship so they can see where they've been. Others place their deck chair at the front of the ship so they can see where they're going."

Then, looking at Charlie Brown, she asks, "Which way is your deck chair facing?"

Without hesitating, Charlie answers glumly, "I can't even get my deck chair unfolded."

Have you ever felt that way? Have you ever had the disheartening feeling that everywhere you look, people are living their lives while you're still fumbling around, trying to get situated?

I certainly have. In fact, my story has sometimes felt like a bathroom mirror after a hot shower: foggy and unclear. One day, my mentor Bobb Biehl gave me a great analogy about living life in a fog. He said that even though a Ferrari is designed to travel over two hundred miles per hour, this high-performance machine can only travel a few miles an hour in a thick fog. In other words, all the horsepower in the world doesn't matter. For the Ferrari to reach its potential, the fog must be lifted.

Are you "idling" while trying to escape from the fog that hinders you from achieving your potential? That keeps you from living your story well?

Let me be clear. There is no ready formula for Clarifying Your Quest. The fog doesn't disappear in an instant. It is not microwaveable nor is it like McDonald's where you become McHappy, McNow. Clarifying Your Quest is a process, not an event, and speed is the enemy of the process. Neither your college nor any organization to which you belong is responsible for developing you into a Page Turner. You are responsible for becoming the person you want to be. If you are to become a Page Turner, you must know your story. Then you must be brave enough to get the supporting cast you need to help you fortify the behaviors you need to develop it.

In my coaching, I encourage CEOs and pro athletes to invest time processing their life as a story and to establish a vision for how they will behave and relate to people. The first order of business is the business of you. Master your story and lead yourself first. Your story becomes clearer over time, not overnight.

To Clarify Your Quest:

- Refuse to Plagiarize Someone Else's Life

- Be Diligent about Your Preferred Story

- Ask Big Questions

- Define and Tell the Story

- Acquire Endgame Foresight

Refuse to Plagiarize Someone Else's Life

I have firsthand experience with this one. Several years ago, my dear friend Adrienne contacted me about collaborating on a consulting job. She had been given a contract to help high-powered women navigate the ins and outs of entrepreneurship and launch their own businesses. She explained what she needed from me. I went to work developing material, concepts, and a training protocol I thought would be helpful and motivational. When I showed my work to Adrienne, she lovingly expressed disappointment with what I had handed her. I will never forget her words: "I hired you for your ideas and your unique insights on leadership, relationships, and human behavior. If I'd wanted to hire John Maxwell for the job, I would've hired him." What I had given her, indeed, amounted to John Maxwell's leadership greatest hits. Excellent ideas from a respected expert, but they did not come from my own heart and mind.

Did I have my own ideas and insights? Sure, I did. But I lacked confidence in my voice. Afraid my work would be rejected, I played it safe. I used a proven person's work instead of exploring what I really believed could most benefit the women I had been hired to help. In essence, I had become an echo and not a voice.

Something similar occurred when I began a major project to complete my doctorate. When I met with one of my professors and explained my initial thoughts and ideas, Dr. Wiater pushed me to dig deeper. What was my quest? What did I want to learn? What did I want to discover? Where did I want to go with my work? What was really churning in my heart? She challenged me to explore and resist the urge to play it safe.

Once again, doing so meant being a voice and not an echo. How tempting to echo someone else's life and work, especially if that work has been successful. How much riskier to pierce the fog, to operate in clarity, to embrace your own heart and voice. And yet how much more rewarding! In her book, Eat, Pray, Love, Elizabeth Gilbert says, "Tis better to live your own life imperfectly than to imitate someone else's perfectly."

Be Diligent About Your Preferred Story

Probable stories unfold when we let life just happen, free-floating down the rapidly moving river of life with no oars or motor, letting the waters carry us wherever they choose and settling on the shore of mediocrity. Preferred stories are the stories we would choose for ourselves. No one "just drifts" toward a flourishing life. Preferred stories happen when we put our oars in the water and steer intentionally in the direction of a satisfying and meaningful life. To live your preferred life, you need a clear vision of where you want to go. Living your preferred story requires you to bring your "best to" whatever you say "yes to."

Living your preferred life is dependent on defining your story, clarifying your mission, and embracing your "why." I reflect on my "why" quite often. In fact, I frequently journal my thoughts about my preferred life. I recently wrote this aspiration: I am intentional about living transparently, treating all people as sacred and leaving them better off than I how found them. But this is my preferred story and my "why." What is yours? When I clarify my story, rowing with purpose toward that destination, I experience deep joy and fulfillment. Clarifying and living your "why" can do the same for you.

Ask Big Questions

The prefix "quest" is part of the word question. A quest is a search, a journey in pursuit of a lofty goal. Questions serve as a catalyst. Along the quest, the right questions can bring laser focus intended to expand your life beyond the superficial. The right questions have a way of stirring up thoughts, ideas and dreams lying at the bottom of the river of your heart and bringing them to the surface. Without regular questions, you will naturally drift in the shallows of complacency. You will wander from the story you want.

Character Questions:

- Am I becoming who I want to become?

- What single value is so important to me that I would teach it my grandkids as the key foundation of a happy life?

- Can people trust me?

Communication Questions:

- What makes me feel appreciated?

- When faced with conflict, how do I like to be approached?

- How do I manage conflict (flee it, fight it, face it)?

- (When faced with conflict) What do you want me to hear, that you feel I am not hearing?

Purpose Questions:

- What do I most want to achieve in the next six months, in the next three years?

- What do I want, what do I want to 'go big on?'? (For family, for relationships, for my business, for myself as a leader?)

Reflective Questions:

- What's becoming clearer?

- In pursuing my goals - do I risk gaining the goal and losing my soul?

- (At the end of the day) What work am I most proud of?

Define and Tell the Story

Whether it is your life, relationships, or business, you must invest time defining and telling the story of who you are and what you wish to contribute to the world. As a Page Turner, you must collaborate with trusted friends, mentors, and advisors to define and refine the story of "you" and how you show up in the world. Businesses that prevail are adept at this. In his book, Built to Last, Jim Collins identifies visionary companies who became great largely due to their clarity about their core values and a core purpose that was non-negotiable. Defining your story and how you show up is based on your core values and core purpose. It must become as natural to you as breathing.

This is the job of the CEO in business and the coach in sports—to define and tell the story. Page Turner leaders wisely collaborate with trusted advisors to define the story, then become evangelists who preach this story through metaphors and storytelling every chance they get. If the story isn't clear, employees and athletes begin to tell their own stories. In my coaching work with CEO's and pro sports teams, I have seen this happen numerous times.

One pro sports team coming off a losing season asked about my services. The general manager got right to the point. He told me about the team's losing streak then asked, "Can you help us get better?" I deliberated on his issues, met him again eight weeks later, and I shared my consulting report. The bottom line? The team had lost its way. The team had gone through a series of head coaches in a fairly short span of time, which meant their "why" kept changing. I advised the team's leadership to hold a private retreat away from the press and fans, to "get into their heart" and address these questions:

- What does it mean to be a (team name)?

- What does it mean to be a player on the team?

- What does it look like to be a leader on and off the field?

- What does it mean to be part of this organization?

As leaders, the general manager and head coach needed to identify and define the story for the organization before they had any chance of communicating that story to the players. The general manager affirmed my observations and immediately went to work. Before long, the coach began moving out players who didn't align with the team story. He brought in players who did fit the story. The manager and coach found ways to communicate that story, even bringing in players from the organization's glory years to help current team members capture a vision of what it really meant to wear that uniform. Two years later this team was in the playoffs.

Acquire Endgame Foresight

An ancient Hebrew proverb says, "It is better to go to the house of mourning than to go to a house of feasting, for death is the destiny of every man; the living should take this to heart." In 2005, Steve Jobs gave perhaps the most memorable commencement speech at Stanford University. He spoke for fifteen minutes and shared what helped him define his story. When he was seventeen, he'd read this quote: "If you live each day as if it is your last, someday you'll most certainly be right."

As Jobs explained to his audience, "Remembering that I'll be dead soon is the most important tool I've ever encountered to help me make the big choices in life … Remembering that you are going to die is the best way I know to avoid the trap of thinking you have something to lose. You are already naked. There is no reason not to follow your heart."

Examining our story through the lens of death can help shape and define our paths and can help bring to the surface what's stirring in our hearts. In fact, at the risk of sounding morbid, one of the exercises I assign to the CEOs I work with is to write their obituaries.

I first realized the power of this perspective when I was about to turn forty and asked myself a heart-centric question, "If I were on my deathbed this very minute, looking back over the course of my life, how would I know if I'd been successful?" From that vantage point, I realized that I would most certainly measure my success based on the quality of my relationships, starting with my bride, our sons, our family, and close friends. And suddenly everything was clear. If at the end of my story, I am going to measure my success by the quality of my relationships, then this mission, this question, this "why" needs to define the story I choose to live today.

From that moment, my story changed. My marital story changed, and one of the first changes was starting a new tradition—a date night every Friday. My parenting story changed, and I began to take my sons on business trips with me. One year, I invited each of my sons to pick a place they wanted to go and have fun, just the guys.

My leadership story changed. For example, as the director of a group designed to impact men as leaders, fathers, and husbands, I started regular individual coaching sessions with my team members. We have regular team meetings to define and reinforce our story, our mission to impact men.

My story changed when I turned forty. And when my story changed, my life changed, too.

What about you? There is simply no better day than today to define your story. Clarify Your Quest. Start living the life you will want to have lived when you come to the last page and look back.

Staying Centered

Even after you have gone through the process of Clarifying Your Quest—you must remain diligent about your preferred story and monitor your life to stay centered. Life happens. People will challenge your beliefs and values. Some will offer you the script they think you should be living. You will even have moments when you question your calling, your dream. You must keep coming back to center.

At my seminars, I illustrate this by placing a bottle of water on the corner of a table. I invite two participants to come forward and ask them to place the bottle at the center of the table. After they place the bottle in the center, I move it and ask them to place the bottle in the center again. I do this several times, and they keep bringing the bottled water back to the center. I ask them, "What is the point of the exercise?" One woman came up to me after the seminar and said, "Many times, I adjust to where other people have placed the water bottle and try to live my life from where they placed me." When leading this exercise on another occasion, after I had moved the bottled water several times, a woman blocked me from moving it again. The audience laughed. I could not have scripted it any better. I told the audience, "You must block people who try to move you off center from the story you desire to live. You must steer around obstacles and challenges since life is dynamic, not static. You must keep your story on course.

A Story Comes to Life

When Jewish psychiatrist Victor Frankl was arrested by the Nazis in World War II, he was stripped of everything—property, family, possessions. He had spent years researching and writing a book on the importance of finding meaning in life—concepts that later would be known as logo therapy. When he arrived at Auschwitz, the infamous death camp, even his manuscript, which he had hidden in the lining of his coat, was taken away. Through grueling hours of manual labor and sleepless nights in filthy barracks, Frankl pondered the meaning of his own life, fighting severe depression and desperately wondering about his future. While working the brutal conditions of the Nazi concentration camp, Frankl described his discovery of meaning amid extreme suffering:

We stumbled on in the darkness, over big stones, and through large puddles, along the one road leading from the camp. The accompanying guards kept shouting at us and driving us with the butts of their rifles. Anyone with very sore feet supported himself on his neighbor's arm. Hardly a word was spoken; the icy wind did not encourage talk. Hiding his mouth behind his upturned collar, the man marching next to me whispered suddenly: 'If our wives could see us now! I do hope they are better off in their camps and don't know what is happening to us.'

In a position of utter desolation, when man cannot express himself in positive action, when his only achievement may consist in enduring his sufferings in the right way—an honorable way—in such a position man can, through loving contemplation of the image he carries of his beloved, achieve fulfillment.

Later, Frankl reflected on his ordeal, in his book *Man's Search for Meaning*, "There is nothing in the world that would so effectively help one to survive even the worst conditions, as the knowledge that there is a meaning in one's life. He who has a 'why' to live for can bear almost any 'how.'"

Few of us will endure the extreme hardships that Frankl went through. Still, his primary thesis should resonate as we contemplate the direction of our lives. Answering the why of our existence will largely inform how we choose to turn the page and write our personal story. Ponder deeply why you're doing what you're doing, and you'll take a giant step in the direction of your destination. Clarify Your Quest and your life story can come into brilliant focus.

Point of the Story

- Refuse to Plagiarize Someone Else's Life

- Be Diligent about Your Preferred Story

- Ask Big Questions

- Define and Tell the Story

- Acquire Endgame Foresight

Developing Story

Screenwriters will tell you that the real work—the hardest work—is storyboarding, i.e., planning out how the story will be told. They must be clear about how all the strands of the plot will tie together before they begin writing. If you've watched behind-the-scenes features for your favorite TV show or movie, you might have seen the writers bent over white boards plastered with Post-It notes or 3x5 cards to organize the scenes—adding, removing, adapting—until they create the seamless sequence they're after.

Your challenge is much the same. Turn off your electronics. Walk on the beach. Wander in the woods. Hole up somewhere quiet. Listen closely to what your heart and soul are telling you. Pray and meditate.

Exercise #1

Listen to Steve Jobs' Stanford University commencement address and write key takeaways in your journal. http://news.stanford.edu/2005/06/14/jobs-061505/

Exercise #2

P—Personality. What is your temperament? What are your main personality traits?

A—Aspirations. If the dream inside of you were never to come to fruition, what might the world have lost?

G—Gifts. What are your unique gifts and skill sets?

E—Experiences. How have your life experiences equipped you to live out your life story from this point forward? What positive experiences propelled your forward? What painful experiences taught you valuable lessons?

Exercise #3

Back to the Future

This is an exercise where you imagine living your preferred story. Take slow, deep breaths and relax. Allow yourself to be creative. Pretend the time is ten to fifteen years from now, and you are living your preferred story. Write a letter to someone special in your life (a parent, a grandparent, a friend, a mentor); write in the past tense and identify the steps that enabled you to be where you are. Here's a sample of what my bride Lezlyn and I wrote to my grandfather...

> Dear Grandpa,
>
> It is 2026 and Turn the Page is having an impact on every continent. We have just installed our fifth clean water system in a small village in Africa. We are planning our 10th annual Page Turners' banquet to honor leaders in sports, business, marriage, and the faith-based community for how they help others live a better story.
> We love you, and we miss you.
>
> Johnny and Lezlyn

Will your preferred story and dream happen as you imagine it? Although it may not happen this way at all, the goal is simply to stretch your imagination, get your dream juices bubbling, and consider the steps that could lead to your goals.

ACT II

Design: Align Your Story

On your tombstone will be a birthdate—dash—death date; what will you do with your dash?

I score high on creativity on nearly every personality scale. That's a good thing. But my challenge is that I often I lack structure. My life was sometimes out of alignment. I believe in structure but have feared that structure would hamper my creativity. But as a result of ignoring structure, I could become scattered and at times reckless. A dream needs structure. I read this quote by Stanford's Bill Burnett, "You don't find your life, you design your life." In fact, a dream without structure leads to sleepwalking —moving aimlessly. Zeal without knowledge is reckless. Be relentless, but not reckless, in pursuit of your dream. By design, I am speaking of being intentional about aligning your life with Championing Generosity and Engaging Community. My story began to get great as I focused on esteeming other people and being vulnerable with my wife and with a small group of supportive men.

Two elements are vital for your dream to be robust: Champion Generosity and Engage Community. A dream featuring you and me as the "star" of the story is a nightmare.

With Champion Generosity, Page Turners strategize to use their gifts and skill set to serve others. They aim to impact more than impress. With Engage Community, the Page Turner shares his/her dream with safe people, a supporting cast of mentors who can help shape their future. Without Engaging Community, you are alone. Isolation becomes a greenhouse for dysfunction and negativity to grow.

Page Turners realize they cannot know themselves, or grow themselves, by themselves. They need a community of caring people to help bring their dreams to life.

Chapter Six

Champion Generosity

"There is no exercise better for the heart than
reaching down and lifting people up."

John Holmes

Breaking Story: Go Give and Get Great

In nearly every blockbuster movie, the protagonist embraces generosity and adds tremendous value to the life stories of others. In the *Sound of Music*, Maria adds value to the Von Trapp family. Her songs, sense of fun, and emotional authenticity transformed their household. In *Braveheart*, William Wallace adds value to the people of Scotland through his valor and patriotism. The legendary Harriet Tubman was not content to free herself only but braved re-enslavement to share her hard-won freedom with hundreds of others. The most powerful stories involve a protagonist who offers or sacrifices themselves for the good of other people. Through their personal investment in others, they realize their own potential.

To live a great story filled with adventure means leaving others better off than how you found them. This is the heartbeat of the Page Turner. Giving develops greatness.

One day I got a call from Mitch. He and I had completed our doctorates together and had enjoyed many motivating conversations about things that mattered during our residency days. Since then, Mitch had helped me out on several occasions, coming to my assistance with his knowledge about, and certification in, various tools including DISC (a personality assessment) and 360 assessments (i.e., evaluations from supervisors, peers, and subordinates).

Now the tables were turned. Mitch needed my help on his book project. I agreed. But in the coming weeks and months, I dropped the ball. I was so bogged down in my own work that I neglected to make the time to add value to his work.

I had no idea how disappointed he was until I called him months later to ask for more information about one of his assessment tools. During our conversation, Mitch told me directly how let down he felt by my negligence and lack of follow through.

It hurt ... I had to ask myself hard questions. Why had I been so willing to accept his help through the years, but so slow to return the favor? I had to admit that despite wanting to believe better of myself, I was operating according to an underlying belief that since helping others didn't get me ahead, I didn't have time for it.

There was another excuse I used not to help others. Not only was I too focused on getting ahead myself, but I was also too fixated on my slights and offenses. Whenever I was feeling emotionally injured over something that had occurred in my life, I would let appointments and commitments drop. I justified my flakiness by thinking, "You don't know what I've gone through. I'm emotionally injured, and you just have to understand."

Both excuses: "I'm too busy to help you" or "I'm too hurt to help you" were a symptom of the same disease: the "It's all about me" disease.

My conversation with Mitch was hard medicine to swallow. But it did get me thinking deeply about my selfish assumptions. My work in turning my own pages hasn't been easy but full of trials and tests. This page, Champion Generosity, has been perhaps the hardest for me to turn. I have struggled to contain an internal war with fear and envy. I have feared that others would get ahead of me, and I have had to fight my envy of those with similar callings and skills. Outhustling them fixed my attention on myself, not on who I was called to be and those I was called to serve. I was operating from a place of insecurity. My motives were impoverished. I was giving only to obtain love but not out of love. I was seeking validation.

Moving away from this unlovely state of mind and turning the page meant learning what it was to be loved by God and be loved in healthy relationships. Only through opening myself to love could I really love and serve others from a wholesome place without trying to be them.

Something else happened around that time, and this experience too challenged my selfish way of thinking.

During a weekend getaway, my wife and I were having breakfast when we had the pleasure of being served by one of the friendliest waiters I have ever met. Isaac appeared to be in his sixties and spoke with a strong Middle Eastern accent. It was evident right from the beginning that Isaac loved people. He shared stories of famous people he had served, stories of his family, and—eventually as we engaged him in further conversation—stories of a very personal challenge he had faced. Isaac was diabetic and, after having two toes amputated from his right foot—struggled greatly with balance. Returning to work after his surgery, he sometimes spilled drinks on customers because he had lost his balance. But he continued waiting tables and made adjustments. In time, he developed more strength in his left foot. He learned how to lead and serve from what had been his weaker foot.

This man's story, told without a hint of self-pity or indignation, forced me to hold a mirror up to myself. I had been through nothing even close to what this fellow had endured, and yet I often fell into a woe-is-me attitude. I grumbled and complained about my lot in life—usually not aloud, but in my mind and heart. I was sure this negative self-talk leaked out in my behavior.

Isaac, unlike me, didn't use his hurts as excuses to disengage. He had stayed engaged, worked hard, adjusted, and remained focused on investing himself in his job and in the lives of those he encountered.

His story made me think of professional athletes, in particular, one future Hall of Famer with whom I'd had the privilege of working. Despite his injuries, he had charged onto the field to give his best. He and other dedicated men had, like Isaac, been living examples of what it means to "play hurt."

Champion Generosity is a Choice

In previous chapters, I've asked you to spend time focusing on your story. And yet writing your best story means understanding when to focus on the stories of those around you. You must know when to put the best interests of others above even your own.

Here's what Cheryl Bachelder, CEO of the Popeye's restaurant chain, says on this subject. Admitting that it's not conventional thinking to put others first, she emphasizes we must do it anyway, grappling, if we must, with "our inner two-year-old." She explains that to be a strong leader, "I need to know you, grow your capability, understand you, and help you reach potential you didn't know you had."

Champion Generosity means being there for the people you lead, serve, live with, and especially love. It means understanding the story they want their lives to tell, and helping them tell that story. Champion Generosity is leaving others better off than how you found them.

When Champion Generosity is missing, the result is troubling. A lack of care directed toward others frequently comes from "scarcity thinking," which in turn is rooted in fear, a fear that there isn't enough room for everyone to grow or be nurtured, so it's "every man for himself," "I'll get mine, and you get yours" and stems from a competitive drive to get ahead regardless of the cost, seeking greatness by demanding recognition or resources—alienating those around you.

Instead, Champion Generosity acknowledges others are an integral part of your story; contributing to their growth develops you and does not diminish you. You must cultivate a mindset of cheering on others as they race toward their dream. Someone else's advance does not mean your setback. It is easy to view others who have similar callings and skill sets as your competitors. I realized instead of pitting myself against them, I could encourage them and affirm their work. I could learn from them. So, take the high road and start training yourself to view others as teammates. You can admire and learn from them and not try to be them. Don't waste time and negative energy blowing out their candle so yours can shine brighter.

The good news is that Champion Generosity is a choice. You can either be a fragrance or an odor. When we are a "fragrance," we bring happiness wherever we go. When we are an "odor," we bring unhappiness whenever we go.

We have a choice.

Page Turners are Generous with the Spotlight

My wife and I travel often, and so, we are highly dependent on, and therefore highly alert to, customer service—at restaurants, hotels, and businesses. We have become sensitive to this even close to home. For example, when my son took his driving test, he wasn't sure he'd passed when he drove the car from the road test back to Department of Motor Vehicles. When he parked, he was given a piece of paper and told to go inside and get in line. No one ever told him, "Congratulations, you passed!" The driving examiner had performed merely the minimum service. I once went to meet with the teachers at my son's school but couldn't find the classroom. Someone in the hall led me to the assistant principal's office. When the school employee introduced me, the assistant principal in a gruff Ebenezer Scrooge voice said, "What do you want?" I have to tell you my son is no longer at that school and, in fact, neither is that assistant principal.

I don't want to sound too critical. I know that I too can be guilty of complacency, of providing perfunctory service in my work and becoming so absorbed in my own activities that I view clients, colleagues, family, or coworkers as a nuisance or interruption. I have to fight this tendency like a sickness. This same sickness affects doctor's offices, where receptionists alienate patients; exists in restaurants, where waitresses leave dissatisfied customers; sinks businesses, when employees drive away clients, destroy brand loyalty, and limit profitability. Indeed, doing the bare minimum affects business: seventy percent of buying experiences are based on how the customer feels they are treated. Indifference and doing the minimum not only diminishes commerce—but sucks the life out of people too.

By contrast, I point to Jenny, who remembers my name and smiles when I order from my local Panera Bread. Cornelius, my barista at Starbucks, greets me and starts a conversation while making my drink, and everyone else's drink. He doesn't forget his patrons, and at Christmas, they don't forget him, dropping off little gifts and desserts in recognition of the regard he gives to all.

Page Turners are generous in serving; they don't just serve drinks, sell tickets, or dispense band aids at the clinic—they give their best and always remember that they are serving people.

They intentionally:

- Treat people with love and honor, whether deserving or difficult. They adopt a mindset that spurs them to leave people better off than they found them.

- Emphasize their interest in others rather than trying to be interesting themselves.

- Add delight to the stories of others. Exceed expectations and create a positive emotional reaction. Become a cheerleader in someone's life and help them step triumphantly over life's obstacles.

- Listen to people by allowing space for them to share their story.

The Benefits of "Champion" Generosity

Generosity is so potent that it not only has the power to change the lives of those around you but to change your life as well. Here are three benefits of living generously:

1. **Your brain craves generosity.** Neuroscientific studies reveal that ninety-eight percent of people have the cognitive ability to empathize with others—that is, to understand their needs. Furthermore, we are not only hard-wired to care, but our brains enjoy it. A study by Jorge Moll and Jordan Grafman showed that when volunteers placed the interests of others before their own, their generosity activated reward centers in the brain, the same centers that activate in response to food and sex.

2. **Generosity enriches marriage.** Couples who are generous in small ways such as making their spouse a cup of coffee, giving a back rub, forgiving each other, or speaking a kind word, feel happier in their marriage, according to the National Marriage Project. Terri Orbuch, project director of the largest and longest running NIH-funded study of married and divorced

couples, also talks about emotional generosity as one of the "best marital life insurance policies. Consistent generosity toward your spouse keeps marriage strong and vibrant over the long haul."

3. **Generosity at work boosts happiness at work.** Altruism at work improves wellbeing. Altruists in the workplace are more likely to help fellow employees, to be more committed to their work and are less likely to quit. Donald Moynihan at the University of Wisconsin says, "Our findings make a simple but profound point about altruism: helping others makes us happier. Altruism is not a form of martyrdom, but operates for many as part of a healthy psychological reward system."

Are you convinced yet? Good. You may ask, what exactly does Champion Generosity look like?

Real Stories

Let me begin by telling you about a time I was on the receiving end of an act of generosity that made such an impact I still savor it years later. While making a presentation at an event, I found myself seated next to Suzan Johnson Cook, US Ambassador. We engaged in congenial conversation about our work and eventually moved on to talk about our families. As parents of teenage boys, we found ourselves exchanging stories of the highs and lows of raising sons. Before we parted ways, the ambassador and I exchanged business cards—you know, as a polite way to wrap up our conversation.

Or so I thought!

A week later, I received an email from this ambassador praising my work and offering encouraging words to me as a father. Here was someone immersed in demanding work with global implications who engaged so fully with my story that she took the time to send encouragement a week after our interaction. By doing so, this ambassador became more than a witness to my story, she became a part of it. Sending a card for no reason, spotlighting someone else's accomplishment or success story on your social media or website, or even paying someone a sincere compliment in front of mutual colleagues are all ways to be generous.

Listening is generosity too. Every heart yearns to be heard. In fact, research by Marshall Rosenberg, founder of Non-Violent Communication, shows that listening is so powerful employee-employer disputes are resolved fifty percent more quickly by the simple act of both parties repeating what they "heard the other say" before responding.

Learning "Champion Generosity" the Ritz-Carlton Way

They say you get what you pay for, and nowhere is this truer than when it comes to staying at a Ritz-Carlton. Occasionally my work has allowed me the joy of luxuriating in one. And every time I do, I experience what I can only call Champion Generosity.

Once I was sitting by the fireplace reading a book when a manager approached and asked, "Would you like coffee and a bagel?"

Caught off guard, I asked, "Is it free?"

He smiled. "Of course!"

Within ten minutes, he returned with a toasted bagel, butter, and a variety of jams presented on nice china. I found myself thinking, "What just happened here?" That was just the beginning. Everyone, including the concierge, room attendant, and bellhop seemed to know my name. I wondered if they were secretly competing to see who could memorize the names of the most guests.

On another occasion, a staff member politely inquired about my work, and I shared that I was writing a book. My wife and I went on to breakfast and then to the fitness center. When we returned to our room, we discovered a gift bag with a pen, along with a note that said, "Mr. Parker, I hope enjoy your stay with us, and we wish you much success on your book."

Moved by this level of customer service, I sought out one of the managers to learn more about their corporate culture. She explained their "mystique," which is the term they use for what they describe as emotional engagement. Their motto is "We are Ladies and Gentlemen serving Ladies and Gentlemen."

Every employee is encouraged to provide the following Three Steps of Service:

- A warm and sincere greeting. Use the guest's name.

- Anticipation and fulfillment of each guest's needs.

- Fond farewell. Give a warm good-bye and use the guest's name.

Finally, employees are encouraged to embrace twelve service values. I will list the first three:

- I build strong relationships and create Ritz-Carlton guests for life.

- I am always responsive to the expressed and unexpressed wishes and needs of our guests.

- I am empowered to create unique, memorable, and personal experiences for our guests.

You may be thinking, "But, Johnny, I am not the Ritz-Carlton. I don't have the budget or the staff to do the things the Ritz does." Don't miss the point. What I just described is the Ritz's culture. Corporate culture says, "Here's how things are done around here." You have a personal culture. How do you serve and engage?

I might add, by the way, that while the Ritz-Carlton does much as a company to set a high bar for how their staff is expected to interact with others, their hallmark generosity is delivered—and experienced—on a very personal, one-on-one level of interaction. It is not handed down from a corporate entity but delivered by a single staff person to a single customer at a time.

So perhaps there are things we can learn from their example, after all.

How intentional are you about incorporating Champion Generosity in your own life? Are you intentional enough to write down the principles by which you choose to operate? Are you committed enough to carry a wallet-size Page Turner's card to remind yourself to listen to those around you, understand their stories, and leave them a little closer to living their dream story as a result of their interaction with you?

Whenever I do Turn the Page seminars for salespeople, I share this quote that I read somewhere: "A sale is not something you pursue. It's something that happens to you while you're immersed in serving your customer." I put it to you that the best life stories, the greatest successes, are things that happen to us while we are immersed in serving those around us.

The Generous Organization

Generosity can be expressed person to person, and person to customer, but can also extend to the organization, i.e., to employees. The old story of 'command and control' in organizations is being replaced with the new and trending story of 'connect and collaborate.' Traditional management models are often authoritative and hierarchical. Orders are issued, and rewards are given as simple transactions. This is seen as the path to inducing productivity. In the 21st century, however, the organizational culture can be quite different. In the new working world, most employees do not respond well to micromanagement and top-down communication.

The Page Turner turns this dynamic on its head, communicating in transformational ways—connecting and collaborating, appreciating employees, working with teams to achieve the vision and providing continued and supportive feedback. The pyramid illustrates this point. The top of the pyramid represents the old story—the leaders use command and control to enforce orders and micromanage subordinates at the base of the pyramid.

In the new story of the Page Turner, the pyramid is inverted with the Page Turner at the bottom point and the subordinates at the top. The Page Turner's focus is to take a coaching approach, leaving people better off, acting as a foundation for their growth.

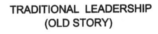

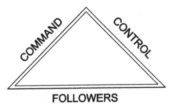

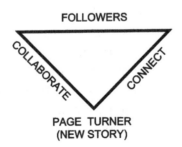

A Story Comes to Life

An anthropologist had been studying the habits and customs of a tribe, and when he finished his work, sat to wait for transportation that would take him to the airport to return home. The children of the tribe had always surrounded him during his time there, so to help pass the time before he left, he proposed a game for the children to play. He'd bought lots of candy and sweets in the city, so he put all of it in a basket with a beautiful ribbon attached. He placed the basket under a tree and then called the kids together. He drew a line on the ground and explained they should wait behind the line for his signal, and when he said "Go!" they should rush over to the basket. The first to arrive would win all the candies.

When he said "Go!" they all unexpectedly held each other's hands and ran off toward the tree as a group. Once there, they simply shared the candy with each other and happily ate it. The anthropologist was very surprised. He asked them why they had all gone together, especially if the first one to arrive at the tree could have won everything in the basket—all the sweets.

A young girl simply replied: "How can one of us be happy if all the others are sad?"

The anthropologist was dumbfounded! He had been studying the tribe for months and months, yet it was only now that he really understood their true essence ...

This story can be found in blogs, Internet articles, and TED talks, referring to the potent concept of ubuntu.

Nelson Mandela translates the meaning of ubuntu this way: "A person is a person through other persons," or "I am because we are." In his explanation, Mandela touches upon the ... multi-faceted nature of ubuntu, as well as the way one feels ubuntu as an innate duty to support one's fellow man. "People should enrich themselves, meaning grow in their own ubuntu, but true enrichment will naturally align with the duty to act toward the spiritual growth of one's community."

Point of the Story

- Leave others better off than how you found them
- Champion" Generosity is a choice
- Champion Generosity confers emotional and mental benefits
- Champion Generosity is the new story in today's organizations

Developing Your Story

Everyone knows what a flashback is in filmmaking parlance—a scene set at a time earlier than the present story takes place. A flashback might show a character at a younger age or illuminate details that led to present-day events. Less common but still used sometimes is a "flash-forward," a scene that temporarily takes the story forward in time, projecting ahead of the current narrative. Here are ways to examine your concept of generosity:

1. Flash back to the people and events that shaped you. The family in which you grew up might have been the kind that did anything for anyone. Perhaps the religious tradition prevailing when you were growing up emphasized giving as a high virtue. Maybe you were the recipient of people's generosity when you needed it most. Then again, perhaps none of these were true for you. If you grew up experiencing neediness, then this also may color your experience, making it difficult

to give or receive from others. Understanding how your experience of generosity has shaped your story, how do you want to move forward?

2. Next, flash forward. In what ways can you choose to be a champion of generosity in your family's, coworkers' or friends stories? How might you demonstrate this today, tomorrow, next week, a month from now, or a year from now? Envision specifically how your generosity would be manifested.

Chapter Seven

Engage Community

"You can't know yourself,
grow yourself, by yourself."

Breaking Story: 'We' Makes a Better 'Me.'

In many noteworthy films, the protagonist never overcomes obstacles and realizes their goals without a mentor, guide or coach. In *It's a Wonderful Life*, the angel Clarence guides George Bailey to a new perspective on his place in the world. In *The Sound of Music*, Mother Superior coaches Maria toward her true calling. In *The Karate Kid*, Mr. Miyagi teaches Daniel how to overcome adversity and pursue honor and self-reliance.

Viggo Mortensen, the actor who played Aragorn in *The Lord of the Rings* movies, was asked what he had learned from being an integral part of the trilogy. He answered, "The lesson is the union with others is more significant than your individual existence. It doesn't deny the importance of your individual existence; it just means that you are a better person the more you connect with others. You're going to know more, you're going to be stronger, and you're going to have a better life if you get over yourself."

I was reminded of the importance a supporting cast when my ophthalmologist diagnosed me with glaucoma. I had to allow my doctor to apply numbing ointment so she could assess my eyes from multiple angles, using a formidable array of instruments to get an accurate diagnosis. In this case, the doctor was my supporting cast. I literally needed her outside insight to help me see clearly. Glaucoma left untreated leads to blindness. Each night, I must use Lumigan drops in my eyes to prevent progression of the disorder. Not having a supporting cast causes you to be blindsided, impairs your life vision and prevents you from turning the page.

This is what a supporting cast is meant to do. They help you see what you don't see and what you need to see. They hold you accountable and call you to live your best story. They serve as human guardrails to keep you from going over the cliff and help you stay on the road toward your destiny.

I had just returned home from the Department of Motor Vehicles, where my son failed his driving test for the second time. That same morning, he had been so excited and hopeful—this would be the day he earned the right to drive! But as I saw his profile in the passenger seat when the instructor drove him back to the building, I knew the worst had happened. And then when he got out of the car, the look on my son's face and his body language spoke loudly and clearly: it was if the wind had been knocked out of him. I felt his disappointment. I put my hand firmly on his shoulder, silently urging him not to give up.

Later, when we walked into the house together, my wife and other two sons, who readily saw what must have happened, rallied around him with encouraging words. We became the supporting cast, bringing hope to a discouraging circumstance. At that moment, my son needed relationship. He needed encouragement. Had he been facing this turn of events in isolation and without a caring person nearby, he may well have internalized the disappointment and lost heart. What a difference it makes when we are buoyed by a supporting cast who walks with us through the traumas and trials of our stories.

Similarly, I was working as a consultant in a dream opportunity for an organization with global recognition. I worked with C-suite leaders on ways to change their corporate culture in a positive way. I provided consulting reports, analysis charts—the whole works, and they implemented my ideas. But two months later, the organization hired a new CEO who sought a 'clean slate.' His new mandate held sway, and I was out. I frequently meet with a group of leaders who share challenging life and leadership stories—my supporting cast. While I was going through this loss, I attended a group session where the group facilitator asked each person the question, "What is your intention?" In other words, "What's your intention regarding where you are in your life?" This question went right to my heart and soul. I was stuck in a chapter of bitterness. I was faced with Demanding Bold Truth about my situation and could decide to pursue emotional health and a better story. Or I could continue in my bitterness. I allowed the group access to my backstage and shared my situation. Working with my supporting cast gave me fresh strength to grieve, and the resilience to turn the page, start a new chapter, and write a better story.

Page Turners Have Emotional Needs ... and It's Okay

I have to admit that allowing other people to walk alongside me when I am feeling disappointed, upset, or vulnerable was not always one of my strengths. A few years ago, I was invited to speak to a group of pro athletes, mostly NFL players and former Olympians, who were retiring from their sport. On the podium with me was another presenter, psychologist Dr. John Townsend. As Dr. Townsend addressed the audience, he listed the basic emotional needs that leaders have and emphasized the importance of having a 'life team'—a support group. We all have emotional needs, he explained, and we all need relationships to help us meet our need for acceptance, affirmation, empathy, love, and perseverance.

What he described was not news to me. After all, I have spent nearly thirty years counseling and coaching, and I have done plenty of emotional intelligence trainings in the process. However, I especially appreciated Dr. Townsend's transparency as he talked about how he himself often neglected sharing his own emotional needs with others.

Listening to Dr. Townsend's openness, I was hit hard by the fact that I too had failed to assemble my own life team, my own supporting cast. I had close friends, but I had been hit-and-miss at revealing my emotional needs to those who cared about me.

Also in attendance that day was the CEO of a billion-dollar, four-hundred-employee business. He spoke up with the very words I'd been feeling but was too embarrassed to say: "I fall short in expressing my emotional needs with a safe group of people. I am accustomed to being the answer guy for everyone else."

I could relate all too well! I scolded myself, "Johnny, you know better. You teach relationship skills; you know the dangers of isolation." And yet, somewhere along the way, I had closed myself off, and I was now paying the emotional price. When I suppress emotions instead of processing them with a supportive, caring cast of people, my emotions inevitably spiral toward shame, negativity, depression, and even spark panic attacks.

I wondered, "Why don't I practice what I teach? What keeps me from soliciting support and input from my supporting cast?" The honest answer? I didn't want to appear needy. I didn't want to feel vulnerable. I was afraid of trusting completely and risking betrayal. So, I'd kept my sharing on a "water ski" level, avoiding "scuba diving" with people who cared.

Why do so many men, in particular, shy away from revealing their emotions to those who care for them?

Of course, one reason is that, historically, the vast majority of boys in the United States have been socialized differently from girls. For example, if a little girl falls and scrapes her knee, she's usually held and comforted. If a little boy falls, he's told, "Get up, there's nothing wrong with you!" or "Shake it off. Act like a man." Even if he ends up with a compound fracture and blood everywhere, he's praised for minimizing the pain, and if he does not, he is shamed by well-meaning people who believe they are toughening him up for the real world.

Dr. Townsend's presentation on emotional needs and support communities gave me a lot to think about. Returning home, I took my wife to breakfast and confided what I wanted to do differently as a man, husband, father, and leader. Since then, I've progressed in this area. I am much more open to the risks, but also the great rewards of sharing with close friends on a deeper level. I do this consistently with my wife, my sons, and my supporting cast. I discover that it not only brings me greater mental clarity but emotional empowerment as well. If you bury your pain alive, be aware that whatever you do not "talk out" you "act out."

More Reasons to Embrace Self-Disclosure

We really can stop letting our emotions run our lives, leaving us isolated and struggling. As life coach Valerie Burton urges, "Don't let emotions rule you; let them school you." A supporting cast can help you sort out emotions so you can glean the benefit of your experiences without becoming a slave to them. With support, we can choose to live differently and more intentionally going forward. Leadership expert Andy Stanley says, "Giftedness ensures a good start; accountability ensures a good finish." Engaging with Community at this level empowers us to finish well and also makes the journey so much more enjoyable.

Research confirms their views. A survey of research studies shows seventy percent of personal happiness is related to the quality of our relationships with close friends, family, coworkers, and neighbors (Murray and Peacock). One study concluded that close relationships influence happiness, and when you feel connected to other people, you are four times more likely to feel good about yourself (Magen, Birenbaum, and Pery).

Still other research shows that to avoid loneliness, people need only one close relationship. Forming that close relationship, according to the study, required an increasing amount of "self-disclosure"—a willingness to reveal personal issues and feelings. Without self-disclosure, people with friends can still be lonely (Jackson, Soderlind & Weiss, 2000). A similar study echoed these results, finding that students who spent time with many friends were nevertheless still plagued by loneliness, which seemed related to their tendency to talk about impersonal topics, such as sports and pop music, instead of their personal lives (Wheeler).

Your willingness to connect—really connect—with others may even play a role in how long you live. In his book, *Blue Zones,* Dan Buettner explains that many of the world's longest living people are members of what he calls the "right tribe," a social community who supported and held each other accountable for healthy behavior.

Lonely at the Top

When you don't have a supporting cast, it really is lonely at the top especially. Life is about relationships. As I have said often, you can't know yourself, grow yourself by yourself. Bookmarks convince themselves, "I shouldn't need someone to help me figure me out." With this philosophy, your backstage can become dark and gloomy. This was a plot line in Don's story. As the owner of his company, he was being sued by a disgruntled employee and accumulating defense lawyer fees. He was angry. Don was a member of a small group I facilitate for CEO's and business leaders, in which each member gets mutual support for their personal and professional lives. As Don disclosed his story,

I could easily understand his pain. He had been a champion for his employees and their success and now, being sued made him feel betrayed, and he wanted to recoil. I was able to help him confront his anger and support his battle with trusting again. The group provided Don with allies; he avoided getting emotionally stuck because he no longer felt alone.

How Do You Build a Supporting Cast?

You cannot become a Page Turner without a supporting cast. This cast should consist of people with whom you feel free to be yourself. People with whom you can be totally honest. People with whom you can be transparent and vulnerable. Engaging with a supportive community creates a judgment-free zone, a place where you can process your shortcomings and failures, and celebrate your successes and potential. These are the safe people to whom you give an access pass to your backstage. Like the Marines slogan, you simply need a few good men (and women!).

Workplaces committed to a healthy culture are recognizing the link between quality employee relationships and business outcomes. Q12 is a tool designed by the Gallup organization to measure the level of employee engagement. Four of the twelve questions target strong workplace relationships:

"In the last seven days, have I received recognition or praise for doing good work?"

"Does my supervisor or someone at work, seem to care about me as a person?"

"Is there someone at work who encourages my development?"

"Do I have a best friend at work?"

We can see that these questions spring from our need for relationship and Engaging Community.

Of course, I can talk all day long about the profound difference authentic engagement with a supportive community will make in your life. But suppose you don't currently have such a cast of characters assembled in your story? What if you have been isolated and guarded for so long that you're not sure whom you can turn to even if you decided to do so?

Take Initiative

A year after I married, I began to realize how alone I felt as a young husband, and how much I lacked confidence in my leadership role at work. I started searching for a group to help me grow as a husband and leader. Just as Luke Skywalker needed guidance in the ways of the Force to become a confident Jedi Warrior, I saw I too needed mentoring to help me reach my potential. So, I hosted a Saturday morning gathering of other newly married men. During that hour, we talked about marriage and leadership. Food greased the wheels (to adopt a line from the movie, Field of Dreams, "feed 'em and men will talk!"). It was an enriching time, and all these years later, I am still grateful for the insights gained and friendships nurtured during that season of my life.

If you're not ready to begin a group, take the initiative to join an existing group. Most churches have study or affinity groups that bring together people with similar interests and goals. You will find that nearly every city and community offers groups for socializing, personal growth, learning a skill, sports activities, and professional development. Additionally, twelve-step groups, through compassionate community and self-disclosure, have empowered thousands of people to escape addictive behaviors, reach their potential, and lead productive lives.

Finally, if starting a group or joining a new group isn't for you, initiate change in the relationships you have with individuals who are currently in your life. Sometimes the first step to developing friendship is simply to be friendlier. The point is, do something.

Find Your Yoda

One of the most memorable characters from **Star Wars**, Yoda is a Jedi Master who mentors Luke Skywalker in becoming a Jedi Knight. Find someone you know who embodies the character qualities you desire, who possesses the meaningful life you desire. Invite that person for coffee, share some of your dreams, and then ask, "Would you be willing to give me some advice?" "Tell me three things you did to create and nurture your success in area X?" "What would you do differently, based on what you know now?"

I sought out seasoned Page Turners and asked them to counsel me. Mr. James coached me on how to be a good husband. Billionaire business owner, Mitch, advised me in business and money management over lunches at a local hole-in-the-wall.

Experienced Page Turners generally enjoy being asked to mentor emerging Page Turners. Don't hesitate to ask them to share their stories and wisdom with you. You benefit whether they meet you for a one-time conversation, or for ongoing guidance. Don't hesitate to connect with those further along the path you want to travel.

Become Yoda to Others

Teaching others the insights you have harvested in your own life is rewarding on many levels. I am now in my fifties and serve as "Yoda" to several promising Page Turners. My wife and I also encourage growth in younger couples. As a mentor, you have the honor of passing along realizations and principles that have been instrumental in your own story. You also have the privilege of creating that safe place for your mentee to process shortcomings and failures, as well as celebrate achievements and milestones, which can be life changing for both of you.

Join a Mastermind Group

Mastermind group members create a collaborative environment to help each person reach their goals. I have been a part of such groups, and they helped sharpen my ideas and introduce me to resources I didn't know existed and kept me accountable for my progress.

One "mastermind" group that enriched my story was called 'The Influentials.' At our monthly meetings, we each had a chance to highlight our work and receive feedback from others. Someone in the Influentials introduced me to a professor at Stanford University Business School who vetted my concept of the 'life as a story.' Interestingly, she encouraged me to take an improvisation class. My wife and I took the improv class together and loved it. We now use improv in our seminars and training. All of this came from my mastermind group.

When stress and pain strike, our inclination is to withdraw from community and isolate ourselves in the backstage of our heart. We wonder and wander in the dark behind heavy velvet curtains. We try to fix and heal ourselves alone. We like to think we are above the 'need' to need.

And yet, the truth is that you will never live your best story in isolation. Writer John Eldredge says, "The deepest part of our heart longs to be bound together in some heroic purpose with others of like mind and spirit.". Find your supportive cast in those who are like-minded and spirited. Your story will be far richer as a result.

A Story Comes to Life

In *The Empire Strikes Back*, Luke Skywalker travels to the Dagobah star system to complete training with Yoda, the last Jedi Master. From the moment he arrives, things don't go as planned for Luke. His ship sinks into a swamp, and Yoda is nowhere to be seen. Or so Luke believes. The only person he meets is an annoying little creature with pointed ears. Luke tolerates him only because he agrees to lead the way to Yoda. But his guide moves too slowly for the impatient young Jedi, who loses his cool.

"Oh, I don't even know what I'm doing here," Luke says in frustration. "We're wasting our time!" Of course, it turns out this creature is Yoda, who sighs and turns away. "I cannot teach him," Yoda says. "There is no patience in the boy ... This one a long time have I watched. Never his mind on where he was. Hmm? What he was doing. Hmph."

Realizing his mistake, Luke pleads his case, and Yoda gives him another chance. From that inauspicious introduction, the relationship between these unlikely allies becomes one of the greatest examples of mentoring in the annals of cinema. Yoda schools—and sometimes scolds—Luke in the physical, mental, and spiritual techniques leading to his Jedi Knight transformation.

Point of the Story

- You can't know yourself, or grow yourself, by yourself

- You need a supporting cast of safe people to help you live your best story

- You need people who love you but who are not overly impressed with you—those who both encourage you and tell you the truth

- Your story is richer when you are connected in meaningful relationships

- A strong supporting cast positions you for flourishing

- Quality time with the right people will strengthen your ability to deal with the wrong people

- As you edit your story for the better—your support cast will also change for the better

Developing Story

1. In what specific ways are you stronger and more effective with others beside you? In what areas of your life could you use more supporting cast members to stay focused on what matters to you? In December 2010, I was entering the final phase of my doctoral program. One morning I journaled this question, "What would I need to finish strong?" I knew having a physical trainer would be crucial for dealing with stress and enable my body and mind to be at its best. I contacted my friend and fitness trainer Marvin Cofield for regular workouts. He became a key member of my supporting cast, and my work with him helped me to graduate on time.

2. Next, honestly assess the sense of community you currently enjoy—or are lacking. Can you use more people in your supporting cast? (And who couldn't?) Make a list of people you might approach to be part of a group, to be a mentor or an accountability partner. Take the initiative and reach out to one or more of these people. Invite them to coffee or to a meal.

3. Adapt the Feed Forward exercise by Dr. Marshall Goldsmith, who helps people solicit helpful ideas and feedback in a group. You can do the same thing by asking people you know to provide their input on a problem or areas of growth that you have. This exercise is geared toward gathering recommendations for

positive changes in your behavior and story. Here are the guidelines …

- Talk to as many wise people as possible

- Talk of your past mistakes, inabilities, and insecurities, i.e., no negative talk of your past

- Don't snap to judgment or critique the ideas you receive

- Review what you have. See how you can apply it in revising your story.

ACT III

Destiny: Master Your Story

"Living, loving, leading happily ever after..."

As a Page Turner, you want to sustain momentum ... and complete what you start. Your story should continually evolve with laser focus toward what you want your legacy to be. Like peanut butter and jelly, destiny and legacy are linked. Destiny is neither an endpoint nor an accomplishment. Destiny and legacy are revealed in your future yet determined by your choices today. Write your destiny and legacy in advance by how you choose to live in the present.

Chapter Eight

Pursue Continual Renewal

*The best stories include pauses
between action sequences*

Breaking Story: Burn On, Not Out

On one of my hikes, I came across a stream that sadly had lost its sound. The water level was too low. Water was there— but stagnant, without movement. No sound. I saw only what it once was.

Your personal wellness affects your ability to flow (upstream) toward your destiny. Page Turners refuse to wait for a crisis to occur to seek renewal. They recognize the need for regular creative downtime to ensure high impact and maximize their efforts. As a Page Turner, you cannot sustain your impact if you neglect to sustain yourself.

Earlier, I shared how each decade has its own unique questions. In your thirties, the question is often, "How can I go as fast as I can to do as much as I can in order to be as successful as I can?" I was living these questions!

In my thirties, my three sons were born; I completed a master's program; launched my counseling and coaching practice; wrote my first book; regularly traveled to speak at conferences and did interviews on *CNN* and *BET*. I was driven to be successful. I entered my thirties passionate and on fire about my work and sense of calling. But at thirty-nine years old, all that was left were dying, sputtering embers.

The problem? I had neglected 'me.' I had taught myself how to work hard, how to network, how to produce results—but hadn't learned how to be emotionally present with myself and fully engaged with people. I'd ignored who I was physically, emotionally, mentally, and spiritually. Physically, I was scraping by on three to four hours of sleep, believing I was getting ahead of those I perceived as my competitors. Emotionally, I was moody and battled panic attacks. As for relationships, my marriage was in a dark place, and my bride and I sought counseling. Mentally, I was scattered and found it increasingly hard to attend to my work. Spiritually, I committed soul abuse, neglecting to care for my real needs, my essence.

At the time, I had no clue what these symptoms meant ... until I received an unexpected call from Tom, one of my mentors. The CEO of a successful company, Tom was a busy man, but he had called just to say hi. His call was like water to a dry desert. He listened intently as I poured out my feelings. Then he said simply, "Johnny, you are burned out."

Within a month, Tom and I, along with our wives, met in Florida and spent time talking and walking the beach. There Tom coached me in how to recognize the signs of stress and burnout. I listened with total attention because I was desperate. I could no longer continue speeding through life toward a non-existent finish line.

Stress Happens

Every material has a breaking point, the maximum amount of pressure or stress it can endure. Highly successful people who neglect Continual Renewal may not want to admit it, but they too have breaking points. Even the most serene men and women can be pressed to the limit. Pressure any material past a certain degree of stress, and it becomes unusable, or it comes apart.

The indicators of burn out are not difficult to detect: easily angered, restlessness, insomnia, cynicism, constant hurrying, depression, anxiety, and decreased productivity. Failing to live an integrated life and constantly driving to get ahead have been linked to heart disease, type II diabetes, and high blood pressure. Consider this equation:

Stress + No Renewal = Burn Out

We are more apt to check the oil level in our cars than our level of spiritual, physical, emotional, relational, and mental wellness. As I discussed earlier, the front stage of our story often dominates our attention. The tyranny of the urgent, and life's hustle and bustle, are overpowering and drown out the still, small voice of the backstage pleading (from behind the curtains) that we listen to our life, to our needs.

It Pays to Replenish

I cannot tell you how many times I have pulled up to Chick-fil-A on a Sunday afternoon only to realize, "That's right, they're closed." I had the privilege of working with this company, and I am simply amazed at their success. This restaurant chain consistently outperforms KFC, Chipotle, Panera, and Dairy Queen, while being open for business only six days a week. Chick-fil-A management is intentional about their core value: allowing employees time to worship, rest, and enjoy time with their families.

Life-work balance is typically a misnomer. The average person will spend approximately 117,000 hours working at their career. There will always be unfinished business in trying to advance your career, have a terrific family life, make time, make time for friends, stay in shape, do chores, and attend social activities. How do you know when you are balanced? Each of these elements cannot be given equal weight. You and I cannot have it all. Life-work intentionality is the way of a Page Turner. It means being intentional about what you really want to go big on—what really matters. Intentionality means keeping your eyes on your legacy and how you want to be remembered. It means realizing no one will read your résumé at your funeral. Life-work intentionality is living with planned neglect—not responding to every text message and not accepting every invitation. You must make choices about how to commit your time. It is asking the question Morgan Stanley asked in their ad, "How do you pass down what you spent your life building up?"

How Does a Page Turner Renew and Restore?

I returned home from my Florida time with Tom and took a one-year sabbatical from traveling and speaking. I stayed active with other things of course, but adopted a healthier pace in order to live a much different story. I latched on to the words of Mark Batterson: "A change of pace plus a change of place equals a change of perspective." This healthier equation replaces the mathematics of burnout:

Stress + Renewal = Burn On

A nineteenth-century businessman wanted to explore the heart of Africa. He hired two African men to guide his tour. He was enthralled with his adventure and moved at a rapid pace on day one and day two. But on day three, as he got up and was ready to embark again, the two African men refused to move from beneath the tree. They explained, "We have been going too fast. We must stay here and allow our souls to catch up with our bodies" This story captures what it means to Pursue Continual

Renewal. To be truly effective in creating our legacy, we must purposely pause to let our souls catch up with our body.

Getting rest produces your best. Just like putting another log on the fire. More fuel feeds the blaze and makes the fire burn brighter. But you and I don't just wander into restful rhythms, we have to be intentional about securing space and time for rest and renewal—that is the challenge. Nature has a rhythm. The sun rises, the sun shines, and the sun sets. God has a rhythm. God created, reflected on His work, saw His work was good, and then rested. To maintain good health, your heart has a rhythm. What's your rhythm? What restores you after you've poured yourself out? There are many ways available.

Use emotional intelligence. Know when the gas gauge on your life dashboard is reading, "Low." Monitor yourself and be aware of signs that your emotional fuel level is depleted, and take decisive action to refuel. Over ninety percent of your success in life is due to being emotionally intelligent and self-aware (Goleman).

Don't cheat yourself of sleep. Aim for seven to eight hours of quality sleep each night. Experts recommend you turn off all technology two hours before bed, make the room as dark and cool as possible, and turn those glowing digital alarm clocks backward, so they don't shine on you. Sleep experts also cite the value of power napping. When you're able to do so, grabbing a fifteen- to twenty-minute nap can invigorate your body and brain with a burst of alertness and energy.

Practice solitude and silence. Solitude and silence are opportunities to withdraw from people, noise, and information overload. I identify with Henry David Thoreau: "I went to the woods because I wished to live deliberately, to front only the essential facts of life, and see if I could not learn what it had to teach, and not, when I came to die, discover that I had not lived." My personal rhythm consists of weekly time alone in the woods to journal, pray, and reflect. There I allow my soul to catch its breath. Once a month, I also schedule a "day-cation" and go to the ocean for a change of pace, a change of place, and a change of perspective. Leadership guru Peter Drucker advises, "Follow effective action with quiet reflection. From the quiet reflection will come even more effective action."

Go fly a kite. That's my way of saying, "Play a little, every day and every week." Play need not be a time-consuming round of golf or a long hike, though there's renewal in either one. You can toss a ball, shoot hoops in the driveway, work out, putter in the garden, wrestle with the kids, knit, do oil painting, color in those grown-up coloring books, or, yes, fly a kite! Playfulness has a way of lifting whatever load you bear and bringing a smile to your heart. Even the Bible supports this principle of play "Laughter doeth good like a medicine" (Proverbs 7: 22).

Find the blessings. They're there. You can find them! Amid the tumult, there are always blessings. When the load pulls you down, look up. What are things, big or small, that you can be grateful for? Find and acknowledge them. Send a quick prayer of gratitude heavenward. You surrounded by thousands—no, millions—of wonderful things. Embrace them, and you'll find your spirits lifting and your load lightening. Your colleagues may even see a grin breaking through. Several successful people I know not only search for and acknowledge blessings, but they also record them in a gratitude journal. Filling the pages with blessings of all kinds doesn't take long. Journaling their gratitude in written form enriches and strengthens the process of finding and acknowledging their blessings. If you go through an especially tough time, you can merely thumb back through the journal of blessings to remember all the good things in life. When bad stuff pulls you down, look up. When life's good, keep looking up. Discover the incredible difference when you consistently and intentionally practice gratitude.

Unplug and disconnect. If you've joined the masses who are addicted to the smartphone, tablet, or laptop, give yourself an intervention! Stop staring at your phone and look at the world around you. Quit babbling into that little box and listen. That strange sound you hear is life—real life. The pleasant chirp you hear is a finch's joyful chatter. The laughter you hear is a toddler discovering his world. When you unplug and disconnect, even for just thirty minutes, you'll discover your world, too. Unplug and disconnect at least thirty minutes a day. You may go through withdrawal, but soon you'll feel a freedom that you've long forgotten.

Breathe. We hear this one so much it seems almost trite. But the breathing principle is so true. Controlled breathing calms your heart rate, your blood pressure, and your emotions. Remembering to breathe can bring you instant renewal. Whenever and wherever you feel tense, or if you simply want to relax a bit, breathe slowly and deeply from your stomach. Inhale for a count of seven, then exhale while counting to eleven. Remember "seven-eleven." Repeat this process at least five times. It works. You can breathe at your desk, during a walk, in the car, or even in a meeting. The deep inhalation oxygenates and refreshes the body and brain; the deep exhalation relaxes the abdominal muscles.

Take a vacation, retreat, or sabbatical. A recent "Fortune 100 Best Places to Work" listed twenty-one companies that offer sabbaticals so people can refresh and renew themselves. I worked for an organization that required each employee to take a three-month sabbatical every five years. Pull out your calendar and look ahead. Pencil in a three-day personal-renewal retreat for yourself. Page forward another three or four months and pencil in another. Now go back and, if you haven't already done so, pencil in that one- or two-week personal or family vacation you've been putting off.

When it's all coming at you too fast, think "WIN." You know the drill. Work demands come in far faster than you can move them out. Meanwhile, responsibilities and problems mount at home. You're pulled in multiple directions, and every direction shouts, "Top Priority!" **WIN** provides a helpful solution, a proven way to stay calm and centered amid the clamor. Pause and ask yourself this calming question: **What's Important Now?** Your answer to this question draws the focus to your true top priority. Concentrate on the task, move the job along, then pose the question again. **What's Important Now?** Focus on that priority until you can move that job along too.

Numerous studies have shown that multi-tasking is not only a myth but virtually impossible. Single-tasking is the way to get things done and done well. **WIN** helps you single-task wisely. **WIN** works on the job, at home, nearly anywhere. **WIN** helps you determine "the one thing" to attend to now and gives you peace about setting aside the rest until you handle the current top priority.

Turning the page from burn out to burn on is so vital to your new life story. If you fail to engage in regular seasons of renewal, you will struggle with weariness and barrenness. If you cannot break away to recalibrate physically, mentally, emotionally, and spiritually, then your work, your home life, and your friendships are going to wither. I have learned that I am not good for people if I am always with people. Deliberately pausing to reset and renew is like a tonic—pausing brings healing and restoration to the weary soul. The rested Page Turner is a breath of fresh air to themselves and to others.

A Story Comes to Life

Two men participated in a wood-chopping contest. The goal was to chop down as many trees as possible from sunup to sundown. The winner would be rewarded great fame and fortune. From early morning to mid-day both men were tied. Suddenly, one of the men decided to pause and take a break. The other wood chopper thought to himself, "The lazy fool, he has probably taken a break for lunch. He's given me a chance to get ahead of him, and I will, without a doubt, win this contest!"

The first woodchopper eventually returned to work and began to chop down more trees than his never-stopping, hungry competitor. By sundown, the man who rested had chopped down nearly twice as many trees as the soaked in sweat, starving, and drained opponent. Bewildered, he asked, "How did you beat me? You were lazier than I and even took a break for lunch!"

"Ah," said the other man, "I did take a break, but during that break that I sharpened my ax."

This story illustrates how we vainly allow the too-busy syndrome to keep us from investing time in renewal. A Hebrew proverb echoes this idea, "Using a dull ax requires great strength, so sharpen the blade." That's the value of wisdom; it helps you succeed. We know in our hearts that we need to break from stressful routines, to recharge physically, mentally, emotionally, and spiritually. But we convince ourselves there's just too much to do and too little time. Like the never-resting wood chopper, we fear to pause a few moments to sharpen the dull ax.

To truly launch your new life story, do yourself a big favor. Be a Page Turner and buck the trend. Go against the grain. Commit to Pursuing Continual Renewal from this day forward. Sure, some exhausted wood choppers out there may look at you funny. Let them. Soon you'll be toppling ten trees to their one.

Through continual personal renewal, you'll feel better, think better, and enjoy a brighter perspective. You'll become a much better spouse, parent, employee, volunteer, and friend. And woodcutter. Why? Because you're taking the time to sharpen the blade.

Point of the Story

- You cannot sustain your impact if you fail to sustain yourself

- Life-work balance is a misnomer

- Life-work intentionality is deciding in advance what really matters

- Stress + No Renewal = Burn Out

- Stress + Renewal = Burn On

- Be deliberate about replenishing once you have poured out

Developing Story

Envision your emotional and spiritual life as the fuel gauge on your car's dashboard. Where is the needle pointing? Full? Half full? Running on fumes? These days, only a minority of people would say "half full" at best, with the majority admitting their tank is empty. Your mission, should you choose to accept it (!), is to get that fuel-gauge needle moving in a positive direction. Ask yourself, "When am I at my best?" "What energizes me?" "When am I most fully engaged?"

Scan the list of restorative habits I suggested. Identify one or two you can incorporate into your life immediately. Select another one or two that you can pursue in the coming weeks and months. Next, customize a "recipe" to fit your own needs and unique situation. What can you add to my list that will enable you to Pursue Continual Renewal? Write down your ideas and post them in a prominent place to remind yourself to do them often.

Chapter Nine

The Next Chapter Begins

Your story is enriched and empowered by the
quality of your (inner) spiritual life.

Three of the biggest heroes in my life are my parents and my
grandfather. My parents are heroic because of their humility
and vulnerability in owning the failure of their marriage and
having the courage and persistence to reconcile and remarry.

My grandfather is a hero because of his wisdom and positive
daily habits. He began every morning praying, meditating, and
reading the Bible. During my high school years, I lived with him
and my grandmother, so I had a front-row seat to his story. He
loved a good conversation, and he always wore white knit socks,
black pants, and a shirt and tie, topped off with a white-and-
black fedora. He said many things that didn't make sense at
the time, but I certainly understand clearly today. I spoke at his
funeral and presented a sampling of his greatest hits:

Saying: "Don't let any grass grow under your feet."

Interpretation: Do not be lazy, keep moving, and get on with
your purpose.

Saying: "You can't holler and swallow at the same time."

Interpretation: You cannot talk, listen, and learn
simultaneously. Either talk and show your ignorance, or be
quiet, humble yourself, and learn.

This last one I deem his greatest of all time. Let me give you
the background that prompted his words. When I was seventeen

years old, I walked into the kitchen one afternoon while he was doing dishes. While he had his back to me at the sink, I jokingly asked him this question, "Pop, how many girls can I date at one time?" He slowly turned around, dried his hands, looked me square in the eyes and answered with the question, "Son, how many hearts do you have?" Here was a man who had only a third-grade education and whose father was a slave. Yet, I'm convinced his daily devotional studies gave him the ability to hone in on what really mattered in most things.

To live your story as a Page Turner means paying attention to what is essential, which means paying attention to things beyond yourself. Looking inward toward your motives, virtues, and vulnerability permits you to extend yourself outward toward strong relationships, productivity, and positive impact. But what about looking upward (God, faith, transcendence)? For many, looking up to God, a higher power, or adherence to a set of spiritual values, something stronger and more enduring than themselves, helps in processing meaning, life, and relationships. As a Christian, my faith helps me put my story in perspective.

I respect wherever you may be in your story vis-à-vis spirituality and faith. You might be a devout person of faith, take a casual interest in such matters, or want nothing to do with traditional faith.

I raise spirituality now because I'm convinced of this: Your spiritual life can be a fundamental part of part of turning the page and taking a giant step toward your dream. I believe, therefore, I'd be doing you a disservice if I didn't share the vital truth that your spiritual life is a reservoir that can sustain you through setbacks, supply you with courage, and provide significance to the investment of your time and talents.

In his book, *Margin*, Dr. Richard Swenson brilliantly captures why spirituality is valuable. He describes the five environments in which we measure progress: the physical, the cognitive, the social, the emotional, and the spiritual. Swenson describes the physical (wealth, the material world) and cognitive environment (knowledge, information) as extremely important. These realms have an advantage because they are visible and most people aggressively focus their energies in pursuit of them.

Nevertheless, Swenson underlines my concept of the frontstage or public world and the backstage or private world when he says, "While the progress we boast of is found within the material and cognitive environments, most of the pain we suffer is found within the social, emotional, and spiritual." The social environment encompasses our families, friends, neighbors, coworkers. Our emotional environment consists of our feelings and attitudes—our psychological state and our spiritual environment comprise the eternal and transcendent—God.

Social media, politicians and *People Magazine* evaluate our status in terms of money, housing, transportation, education, communications, technology, and energy. Yet what about our social, emotional, and spiritual wellbeing; our needs for connection, for love, hope, and for a connection with something more enduring than ourselves?

Over the years, I have worked with scores of individuals on turning the page in their lives, and I found that those who embraced their spirituality accessed an extra measure of power in their quest. Page Turners look to something bigger than themselves for strength, hope, optimism, and resiliency. Moreover, people who seek to step forward on their journey recognize that spirituality imbues their efforts and ambitions with meaning beyond the here and now.

Though concepts and spiritual practices vary, there is no doubt that spiritual matters are vitally important to most people. According to social scientist L.W. Fry, "Spirituality includes two essential elements in a person's life: (a) transcendence of self, manifesting in a sense of calling or destiny, and (b) belief that one's activities have meaning and value beyond economic benefits or self-gratification. A sense of calling and higher meaning fosters the development of certain values, including vision (i.e., defining the destination, reflecting high ideals, and encouraging hope/faith), altruistic love (i.e., forgiveness, kindness, integrity, empathy, honesty, patience, courage, trust, and humility), and hope/faith (i.e., endurance, perseverance, and expectation of reward/victory)."

Your Spiritual Life, a Foundation for Identity

You know by now that I am a passionate advocate of maximizing your potential, pursuing big goals, and working hard to achieve success. Danger comes, however, when we build our identity out of these things, which have nothing to do with who we really are. Jobs can be taken away. Possessions can be lost. Money can evaporate with a stock market plunge. The self-image we create out of these things is no more than a convincing illusion. If you mistakenly believe you are these things, the loss of any one of them feels life-threatening. You could feel unanchored and confused until you discover your true self is more than mere physical trappings.

French philosopher Teilhard de Chardin sums it up perfectly. "You are not a human being in search of a spiritual experience. You are a spiritual being immersed in a human experience." Being attentive to your spiritual life enables you to discover who you really are and help shape your story.

Your Spiritual Life Bolsters Your Wellness

If you key the words spirituality and health into your favorite online search engine, you will be directed to hundreds of pages highlighting a vast array of research studies. Countless times, spiritual beliefs and practices are shown to promote good health and wellbeing. Research investigation shows that a leader's increased engagement in specific spiritual practices, such as prayer and meditation, leads to greater leader motivation

(Alexander, Rainforth, & Gelderloos, 1991), strengthens leader relationships (Anderson et al., 1999), improves leader resilience (Quick, Gavin, Cooper, Quick, & Gilbert, 2000), and increases leadership effectiveness (McCollum, 1999). Persuasive, right? That's why I simply can't neglect mentioning the role of spirituality for the Page Turner.

A Story Comes to Life

At twenty-two, driving home through the Bronx in my mother's black-and-gray 1982 Buick Skyhawk after an evening with friends, my eyelids were heavy. Boom!

I had fallen asleep at the wheel. My car was wrapped around a tree. The Skyhawk looked like an aluminum can someone had stomped on. I sat in stunned silence, with agonizing pain in several places. I spent an entire week in the hospital and another two months on crutches. My beloved Buick was scrapped.

People rarely express gratitude for a car accident. Why, then, am I thankful for that life-threatening wreck? In my hospital bed, for the first time in my life, I confronted my own mortality. I could have died—really died! What am I doing with my life anyway?

Although my family had always emphasized faith in God, I'd never before considered my life's end, and what I would do with my time before that end came. Though it would be nearly two decades later before I intentionally turned the page in my life, that accident got my attention and got me moving in the right direction.

That crash in the Bronx certainly wasn't the only time I have contemplated the meaning of life. I've had other car wrecks, suffered health scares, and attended funerals for close friends who died far too soon. At such times, I rely on my spiritual life for direction. At the same time, I hasten to add, my spirituality isn't important only at times of crisis or loss, but is a day-by-day, moment-by-moment experience. My spiritual life, my faith in God, is a daily source of peace, insight, and strength. My motivation and core values have emerged from my faith, and my spiritual beliefs enable me to persevere and be resilient in the face of adversity.

Throughout this book, I have urged my readers to become Page Turners, that is, to become active agents in leading their lives. By Demanding Bold Truth, they confront their backstage and change their lives accordingly, healing hurts and acting on their strength to realize dreams. By Clarifying Their Quest, they examine their values and determine the shape of their legacy. By Engaging Community, they accept nourishment from others, who hold them accountable and provide objective insight. By employing Champion Generosity, they share the spotlight, contributing to the development and growth of those around them. And by the Pursuit of Continual Renewal, they ensure their story retains vitality and the resources to endure.

These Page Turner concepts have led me through tremendous change. But I say again that a critical element of turning the page for me, one that has made all the difference in my own story, is my reliance on spiritual guidance. Page Turners have a better advantage when they recognize that they are not the sole author of their story but instead, are supported by linking their story with a power greater than themselves.

Harvard Business School has forums where executives from diverse industries gather to discuss the role of spirituality in the transformation of leaders. Increasingly, leaders are finding spiritual principles and deeply held values to be fundamental in achieving their business goals. They incorporate contemplation and mindfulness in charting future activities. They use ethics to shape decisions about the products they make and determine to contribute to human dignity when choosing sponsorships and organizational donations. Some industry leaders confess to having been 'caught up' with a round of profiteering, or grasping for an ever-retreating gold star, stuck on the merry-go-round of "succeeding," that exhausted me in my forties. Christian and Muslim executives, as well as those of other faiths, instead of making their faith something that they leave at home, now pack their spirituality in briefcases and take faith to the office.

They seek fulfillment, rather than mere success, working toward harmony between their "backstage" and "frontstage." They note that their businesses have not suffered, but rather have profited by the infusion of faith, trust in God, and commitment to social justice.

As you embark on the exciting journey of turning the page, I encourage you to regard a spiritual life as a generator of power, repository of wisdom, and source of courage. If you can embrace this wellspring of support and renewal, you will add a dimension of vitality to your story in dramatic ways.

Developing Story

1. If you do have a faith practice, are there ways that you can realize more benefits? Attend services more regularly? Delve more deeply or consistently into study? Discuss and gather with others of like opinion? Resolve to fuel your page turning (frontstage and backstage!) by using your spiritual resources.

2. If you do not have an organized connection to a spiritual practice, spend time contemplating what stimulates you to awe? Gaze at the ocean, contemplate a thunderstorm, or pictures of the planets.

Final Note

I wrote this book because I do not want to die with regret (who does?). Poet Mary Oliver asks the defining question, "Tell me, what is it you plan to do with your one wild and precious life?" As of this writing, I have been alive for 18,753 days. What a blessing! And yet, my life won't last forever. There is a limit to how long you and I will walk this earth. The last thing I want to do is live someone else's story, or live distracted from my calling and miss living my "preferred life" because I allowed fear to terrorize me and hold me hostage.

Each day your life is writing something. When the final chapter of your life comes to a close, how will your life read? Will your life pen something worth reading? What will your life write today? Here's the pencil. Turn to a fresh, new page. Write well.

About the Author

Determined to inspire one million people to live better, brilliant and bountiful lives, Dr. Johnny Parker designed the "Turn the Page" system. Through executive coaching, seminars and keynote presentations, he has a twenty-five-year track record of helping hundreds of CEO's, aspiring entrepreneurs, and leaders experience authentic success by viewing their life/work as a story.

His "Turn the Page" approach has enhanced organizations such as AOL, NFL, Fannie Mae, Colonial Parking, Chick-fil-A, Signature Flight Support, The Department of Homeland Security, University of Maryland at Baltimore County, Tuskegee Airmen, Mary Kay, Smartronix, Kairos, US Army, US Navy, and US Air Force.

Dr. Parker is an adjunct professor at Johns Hopkins University where he teaches Introduction to Positive Psychology, an evidence-based approach that focuses on conditions leading to happiness and flourishing.

Dr. Parker has served as life coach and consultant for the Washington Redskins and Washington Mystics and he regularly helps pro athletes (NFL, NBA, PGA and WNBA) and CEO's develop healthy personal/professional lives and strong relationships.

CNN International and national media such as N*BC News, Viewpoint, BET, Washington Post, Ebony, Essence* and the *Baltimore Sun* have highlighted Johnny's solid message. He is a featured relationship expert in two films—*Still Standing* and *Divorce Care*.

Johnny is the author of *Renovating Your Marriage Room by Room, Faith Like a Child, Exceptional Living: 31 Exercises for Enriching Your Life, Work and Relationships.* He holds an MA in Counseling Psychology and a Doctorate in Strategic Leadership from Regent University.

A native New Yorker, Dr. Parker is married to his best friend, Lezlyn, and they have three sons, JP, Jordan, and Joel, and an energetic Cocker Spaniel, Jay-Jay. The Parkers reside outside Washington, DC.

References

A Note from Johnny

Acuff, Jon. Podcast, Five Leadership Questions. 5LQ Episode 102. LifeWay Leadership.

Chapter One

Angelou, Maya. *I Know Why the Caged Bird Sings*. New York: Random House Trade Paperbacks, 2009. Print.

Jerome Bruner mentioned by Smith, Paul. Lead with a Story. A Guide to Crafting Business Narratives that Captivate, Convince, and Inspire (New York: Amacom, 2012), p. 11.

Dillard, Annie. *The Writing Life* (New York: Harper & Row, 1989), p. 32.

Litherland, Janet. *Storytelling from the Bible* (Colorado Springs, Colo.: Meriwether Publishers, 1991), p. 3.

I heard Brad Lomenick speak at Student Leadership University in Orlando, Florida June 2016.

Jerry Maguire. Directed by Cameron Crowe, performances by Tom Cruise, Cuba Gooding, Jr., Renee Zellweger, Kelly Preston, Jerry O'Connell, Jay Mohr and Bonnie Hunt, Gracie Films and TriStar Pictures, 1996. http://www.livescience.com/40188-dark-history-alfred-nobel-prizes.html.

Chapter Two

Bradberry, Travis. "Why You Need Emotional Intelligence to Succeed." Inc.com, 15 March 2015, www.inc.com/travis-bradberry/why-you-need-emotional-intelligence.

Brown, Brené. *Daring Greatly: How the Courage to Be Vulnerable Transforms the Way We Live, Love, Parent, and Lead.* New York, NY: Gotham Books, 2012.

Maturana, H. and Bunnel, P. "The Biology of Business: Love Expands Intelligence." May 1999, www.academia.edu/7925296/The_Biology_of_Business_Love_Expands_Intelligence.

Cathy, Truett S. *Eat Mor Chikin: Inspire More People.* Decatur, GA: Looking Glass Books, 2002.

Achor, Shawn, 2012 February. "The Happy Secret to Better Work." Retrieved from www.ted.com/talks/shawn_achor_the_happy_secret_to_better_work.

Chapter Three

Drucker, Peter. Leader to Leader Journal. "Managing Knowledge Means Managing Oneself." Spring 2000.

The Pursuit of Happyness. Directed by Gabriele Muccino, performances by Will Smith and Jaden Smith, Columbia Pictures, 2006.

Places in the Heart. Directed by Robert Benton, performances by Sally Field, Lindsay Crouse, John Malkovich, Ed Harris, Danny Glover, and Amy Madigan, TriStar Pictures, 1984.

Muller, Wayne. *Legacy of the Heart: The Spiritual Advantages of a Painful Childhood.* Hodder & Stoughton, 1997.

Nouwen, Henri J. M. *Reaching Out: The Three Movements of the Spiritual Life,* 1986.

I heard Richard Rohr interviewed by Oprah Winfrey on Super Soul Sunday.

Simon, Paul and Garfunkel, Art. "I Am a Rock." Sounds of
Silence. Columbia, 1965.

Souza, Alfred D. "Happiness," www.soulonline.org. Web,
accessed 1 January 2017.

Camp Grounded—www.campgrounded.org.

Susman, Warren. *Culture as History*. Random House Publishing,
New York, NY 2012.

The Truman Show. By Peter Weir, performances by Jim
Carrey, Laura Linna, Noah Emmerich, Natascha McElhone,
Holland Taylor and Ed Harris, Scott Rudin Productions and
Paramount Pictures, 1998.

Chapter Four

Collins, S. (2008). *The Hunger Games*. New York: Scholastic
Press, 2008.

Hall, Kevin. *Aspire: Discovering Your Purpose Through the Power
of Words*, New York, NY, Morrow, p.111-112.

Keyes, Corey L.M. "The Mental Health Continuum from
Languishing to Flourishing in Life."

Journal of Health and Social Research, 2002. Vol 43 (June) p.
207-222.

Seligman, Martin. "Orientations to happiness and life
satisfaction: the full life versus the empty life." Journal of
Happiness Studies. March 2005. Vol.6, pp. 25—41.

Schultz, H., & Gordon, J. (2011). *Onward: How Starbucks Fought
for its Life without Losing its Soul*. New York, NY: Rodale.

Paraphrased from Thompson, Wright "Urban Meyer will be
home for dinner," ESPN The Magazine, August 22, 2012.

Flight. Directed by Robert Zemeckis, performances by Denzel
Washington, Don Cheadle, Kelly Reilly, John Goodman,
Bruce Greenwood, Brian Geraghty, Tamara Tunie, and
Melissa Leo, Paramount Pictures, 2012.

Williamson, Marianne. *A Return to Love: Reflections on the Principles of "A Course in Miracles"*, Ch. 7, Section 3 (1992), p. 190.

Chapter Five

Collins, James C., and Jerry I. Porras. *Built to Last: Successful Habits of Visionary Companies*. New York: Harper Business, 1997.

Man's Search for Meaning, Part One, "Experiences in a Concentration Camp," Viktor Frankl, Pocket Books, ISBN 978-0-671-02337-9 pp. 56—57.

Gilbert, Elizabeth. (2007, c2006) *Eat, Pray, Love: One Woman's Search for Everything Across Italy, India, and Indonesia New York*: Penguin.

Merton, Thomas. *The Silent Life*. Farrar, Straus, and Giroux. New York, 1957.

Steve Jobs: news.stanford.edu/2005/06/14/jobs-061505.

Chapter Six

Bachelder, Cheryl. *Dare to Serve: How to Drive Superior Results by Serving Others*. Barrett and Koehler, 2015.

Moynihan, Donald. "Helping Others Makes Us Happier at Work, Research Finds." Huffington Post, 7/13/2013.

Oppenheim, C.E. "Nelson Mandela and the Power of Ubuntu." Religions, 2012 V.3 p. 369-388.

Orbuch, Terri. http://www.nextavenue.org/generosity-may-be-what-matters-most-marriage.

Zahn et. al (Moll and Grafman). "The Neural Basis of Human Social Values: Evidence from Functional MRI. Cerebral Cortex"; Oxford Journals. 2009.

Pay It Forward. Directed by Mimi Leder, performances by Kevin Spacey, Helen Hunt, Haley Joel Osment, Jay Mohr, Jim

Caviezel, Angie Dickinson, Jon Bon Jovi and Marc Donato,
Bel Air Entertainment and Tapestry Films, 2000.
Yenya, J. The village wisdom messenger. Blog. http://www.
jackyyenga.com/the-soirit-of-ubuntu.

Chapter Seven

Walters, R., Cattan, M., Speller, V., & Stuckelberger, A. (1999).
Proven strategies to wellbeing. Eurolink Age, London.
Murray, C.B. & Peacock, M.J. (1996). A model-free approach to
the study of subjective wellbeing. In H.W. Neighbors & J.S.
Jackson (Eds.), Mental Health in Black America, Thousand
Oaks: Sage Publications, 14-26.
Jackson, T; Soderlind, A. & Weiss, K. Personality traits and
quality of relationships as predictors of future loneliness
among American college students. Social Behavior and
Personality, Vol 28(5), 2000, 463-470.
Magen, Birenbaum and Peri, 1996, cited in D. Niven, 100 Simple
Secrets of Happy People. Hallmark, 2001.
The Empire Strikes Back. Directed by Irvin Kershner,
performances by Mark Hamill, Harrison Ford, Carrie Fisher,
Billy Dee Williams, Anthony Daniels, David Prowse, Kenny
Baker, Peter Mayhew and Frank Oz, Lucasfilm and 20th
Century Fox, 1980.

Chapter Eight

Batterson, Mark. http://www.markbatterson.com/
uncategorized/god-ideas-vs-good-ideas/
Curtis, B., & *Eldredge*, J. (1997). The *Sacred Romance*: Drawing
Closer to the Heart of God. Nashville: T. Nelson.
Drucker, Peter. http://www.dailygood.org/pdf/dg.php?qid=4595
Goleman, Daniel. "What makes a leader?" Harvard Business
Review, January 2004.

Marshall Goldsmith: www.marshallgoldsmithfeedforward.com.
Thoreau, Henry D. *Walden*, Or, Life in the Woods. London: J.M. Dent, 1908.
Claire Newton: www.clairenewton.co.za/my-articles. "The Wood Choppers Contest."

Chapter Nine

Alexander, Rainforth, and Gelderloos 1991, in Psychology, Religion, and Spirituality. J. Nelson.
Springer Science & Business Media, 2009.
Anderson et. al. Encyclopedia of Leadership, 1991.
Fry, L.W. (2003). "Toward a theory of spiritual leadership." The Leadership Quarterly, 14(6), 693-727. http://hbswk.hbs.edu/item/does-spirituality-drive-success, 22 April 2002.
McCollum, S., 1999, in The Roles of Internal Public Relations, Leadership Style, and Workplace Spirituality in Building Leader-Employee Relationships and Facilitating Relational Outcomes.
Quick, J., Gavin, J., Cooper, C., Quick, J., & Gilbert. "Executive health, building strengths, managing risks." Academy of Management Executives, 14 (2) p 34-44, 2000.

Final Note

Mary Oliver, "The Summer Day," in New and Selected Poems, vol. 1 (Boston: Beacon Press, 1992), 94.

51491205R00096

Made in the USA
Middletown, DE
03 July 2019